The Conceptualization of Race in Colonial Puerto Rico, 1800–1850

Rochelle Brock and Richard Greggory Johnson III
Executive Editors

Vol. 47

The Black Studies and Critical Thinking series
is part of the Peter Lang Education list.
Every volume is peer reviewed and meets
the highest quality standards for content and production.

PETER LANG
New York • Bern • Frankfurt • Berlin
Brussels • Vienna • Oxford • Warsaw

KATHRYN R. DUNGY

The Conceptualization of Race in Colonial Puerto Rico, 1800–1850

PETER LANG
New York • Bern • Frankfurt • Berlin
Brussels • Vienna • Oxford • Warsaw

Library of Congress Cataloging-in-Publication Data
Dungy, Kathryn.
The conceptualization of race in colonial Puerto Rico, 1800–1850 /
Kathryn R. Dungy.
pages cm. — (Black studies and critical thinking; volume 47)
Includes bibliographical references and index.
1. Puerto Rico—Race relations—History—19th century.
2. Puerto Rico—Social conditions—19th century.
3. Social change—Puerto Rico—History—19th century.
4. Puerto Rico—Population—History—19th century. I. Title.
F1983.A1D86   305.80097295—dc23   2014016134
ISBN 978-1-4331-2043-5 (hardcover)
ISBN 978-1-4331-2042-8 (paperback)
ISBN 978-1-4539-1363-5 (e-book)
ISSN 1947-5985

Bibliographic information published by **Die Deutsche Nationalbibliothek**.
Die Deutsche Nationalbibliothek lists this publication in the "Deutsche
Nationalbibliografie"; detailed bibliographic data are available
on the Internet at http://dnb.d-nb.de/.

Cover image: *El Velorio* by Francisco Oller

The paper in this book meets the guidelines for permanence and durability
of the Committee on Production Guidelines for Book Longevity
of the Council of Library Resources.

© 2015 Peter Lang Publishing, Inc., New York
29 Broadway, 18th floor, New York, NY 10006
www.peterlang.com

Printed in the United States of America

Table of Contents

Preface: Fusing the Races

I began my studies of slave societies and free people of color in the Caribbean in an effort to better understand my own family history. My paternal ancestors were, variously, Europeans, Africans, and Native Americans, all of whom converged on Virginia shores in the late 1600s. My maternal ancestors, again a mixture of European, African and Native American peoples, forged a life of free status for themselves in the slave states of Louisiana, Mississippi, and Arkansas. Both families share a history of mixed marriages, indentured servitude, migration, and generally working against the space that people of color were supposed to occupy, both during slavery and in its aftermath. I was looking for links to my seemingly unusual heritage of free people of color struggling against the historical tide. Was there a place where a free person of color could own property, land, and/or slaves, and not be an anomaly? Was there somewhere free people of color could live in an integrated community as social equals?

I never found a utopia. In fact, I found places where my relatives, had they ended up there, might actually have found a crueler trajectory in the social and cultural sphere. However, one location I found piqued my interest. Puerto Rico glimmered in the Caribbean Sea with an unusual history surrounding its free people of color. In fact, there was a point in the nineteenth century when the island's population of free people of color actually outnumbered both the European *and* slave populations. What did this mean for civil rights? Economic possibilities? Social interactions? Curiosity grabbed me and I was hooked.

I began to consider the issue of people of African descent in the Americas, the connections between colonial Latin American historiography and the scholarship on the Atlantic World, finding both continuities as well as disjunctures between the two fields of study. The current research on free people of color in the colonial Atlantic World diaspora tends to focus on the United States, the British and French Caribbean, Cuba, and Brazil. Analysis of other regions such as Puerto Rico, Central America, and the Andes offers historical examples of community formation that incorporated legal strategies in secular and ecclesiastical institutions, as well as articulations of multiple African identities. Therefore, it is critically important to expand the framework of the Atlantic World diaspora that has come to shape so much of the recent scholarship on Africans in the Americas.

The rise of Atlantic World history yields a broad geographic scope that challenges concepts of regionality and nationality, focuses on the movement of people and commodities around the Atlantic basin, and brings greater attention to the centrality of the effects of slavery in the culture and the historiography. The field has generated a good deal of scholarship. One of the benefactors of this new attentiveness has been the Caribbean basin, with its myriad nationalities and cultures.

Scholars continue to have difficulty recognizing the links between islands, colonial powers, and nationalities beyond our familiar regionalization of the British Caribbean, the Spanish Caribbean, the French Caribbean, and so on. However, the Caribbean region is bound by a shared history, common characteristics, and complex cultural elements. The island societies were the center of the Atlantic economy of the European powers. This work attempts to expand the regionality and demonstrate how Puerto Rico is a microcosm of the Caribbean at large.

Our knowledge of free people of color, as well as the geographic origin and ethnicity of slaves introduced into peripheral areas of the Americas, such as the former Spanish colony of Puerto Rico, is limited. Information contained in eighteenth- and nineteenth-century census records and in baptismal, marriage, and death registers enables us to locate and identify free people of color in a number of island communities. Drawing upon data culled from archival registers, this study seeks to broaden our understanding of the free people of color in Puerto Rico between the years of 1790 and 1850.

The Conceptualization of Race in Colonial Puerto Rico shows a different perspective as it looks outside of the large municipality of San Juan (the seat of government and the largest city on the island) to view smaller communities on other parts of the island. The perspective on interactions between white and black, free and enslaved, is altered when viewed beyond the cramped quarters of the walled capital, out among the small towns and villages.

This work looks at the population of free people of color in nineteenth-century Puerto Rico by analyzing the ways in which free people of color made choices regarding work, marriage, and the prevailing legal system to construct an island community. This study provides a wider profile of the country's class and social structure, while linking the broader historiography of Atlantic World and Latin American social history and various studies of Puerto Rican urban and rural centers.

The Conceptualization of Race in Colonial Puerto Rico is comprised of five chapters. Chapter one introduces the island and the people to the reader, explains terminology, and begins to focus the lens on the nineteenth century. It illuminates the unique demographics that set this island nation apart from other plantation economies in the Atlantic World.

Chapter two is an examination of the evolving population and politics of early nineteenth-century Puerto Rico within a wider Caribbean and Atlantic context. It considers how cultures in the Caribbean region evolved in different times and places and unfolded in disparate ways. These diverse societies varied in their demographic profiles, the products they exported, their political institutions and practices, and their interactions with the metropole, among other characteristics. The complex interactions found in these disparate locales shaped the societies in which free people of color found themselves living. The chapter also illustrates how cultural influences flowed across Europe and Africa to the Caribbean colonies and affected their political, economic, and cultural growth.

Chapter three utilizes case studies to demonstrate how the construction of identity in Puerto Rico intersects with ongoing debates in African diasporic scholarship regarding the models of continuity and creolization in the Americas. There was considerable diversity in the geographic origins and professions of immigrant free people of color and their counterparts on the island. Few slaves were brought in to Puerto Rico from Africa or from elsewhere in the Americas, and the supply of these was erratic and limited. For the most part, outside of San Juan, there were no endogamous living patterns or professions for immigrant or native free people of color. Commonalities with their white counterparts facilitated integration and promoted social cohesion among the newly arrived free people of color, as well as those already present in the population. It also facilitated their integration into what was emerging as a unified Afro–Puerto Rican community, as well as into the Puerto Rican community at large.

Chapter four explores how free people of color claimed categories of inclusion based on legal and cultural concepts of marriage. By delineating how free people of color negotiated courtship, marriage, and widowhood, one can witness burgeoning group self-awareness. Parental opposition to marriage uncovered conflict over allegedly unequal partnerships within the seemingly endogamous community of free people of color. They utilized parental and state control of sexuality and marriage to safeguard social hierarchy both within their community and on the island at large, revealing heterogeneity previously unaccounted for in Puerto Rico.

Chapter five shows how free people employed their rights as citizens of both Puerto Rico and the Spanish Empire to present themselves as civilized subjects and loyal Spaniards. The growing sense of class and nationality on the island fostered acceptance for free people of color and recognized them as integral members of the society.

The nuances found in Puerto Rico's community of free people of color reflect the development of a racial national consciousness toward an ideology of racial mixture. The white and free people of color on this "island of perfect tranquility" were truly striving to "work together, without regard to color, only to education and social position."[1] The island's unusual demographics allowed its inhabitants the opportunity to approach race relations differently. Free people of color and whites found a way to co-exist without the degree of fear or antagonism found in other plantation societies.

The early nineteenth century saw many changes both in the region and on the island, but the white and free colored inhabitants of Puerto Rico worked steadily toward a previously unrealized compatibility. The manner by which free people of color fit into Puerto Rican society validates the notion of a country striving steadily toward a goal of a "fusion of the races."

Notes

1. (AHN Ultramar 5103, exp. 64, 3 January 1874 at CIH, UPR, roll 164 n.d.).

Acknowledgments

I have accumulated many debts in researching and writing this book about free people of color in nineteenth-century Puerto Rico. They are debts I can never discharge, but here I have the opportunity to acknowledge those who have been so generous in their support of me and of my work.

To my Spelman family who believed from the beginning that I had potential in the historical field. That initial encouragement came from professors Dalila de Sousa Sheppard, Margery Ganz, Jim Gillam, and Michael Gomez. Further molding occurred at Duke University under the guidance of a myriad of knowledgeable and talented people. Thanks to professors Jan Ewald, Ray Gavins, Nancy Hewitt, John Hope Franklin, Karla Holloway, Sydney Nathans, Richard Powell, Anne Firor Scott, John TePaske, Peter Wood, and Dean Jackie Looney. And I would surely have lost my sanity without the encouragement from the wonderful, nurturing cohorts in the Duke Graduate Studies program: Herman Bennett, Leslie Brown, Vincent Brown, Alex Byrd, Rod Clare, Charles McKinney, Jennifer Morgan, Celia Naylor, Peter (Quaku) Pletcher, Stephanie Smallwood, Nikki Taylor, Annie Valk, and others.

As a dissertation in progress and later as a book manuscript, this project benefited from fellowship assistance that allowed me to concentrate on research and writing. I thank the generous support from the Graduate School at Duke University, the Ford Foundation, the New England Board of Higher Education Dissertation Scholars-in-Residence Program at the University of Vermont, the Women's Studies Travel grant at the University of Vermont, the Provost's Faculty Development Fund at New College of Florida, and the Faculty Development Fund at Saint Michael's College.

I am indebted to the librarians and archivists at all the repositories listed in my bibliography, and am especially grateful to the staff at the Archivo General de Indies, Sevilla, Spain; the Archivo General de Puerto Rico; the Centro de Investigaciones Históricas at the University of Puerto Rico, Río Piedras; Biblioteca Lázaro, Colección Puertorriqueña, University of Puerto Rico, Río Piedras; and Durick Library at Saint Michael's College.

The three maps were drawn by the Cartographic Laboratory, Department of Geography, University of Wisconsin.

I finished the manuscript as a member of the department of history at Saint Michael's College. George Dameron, Susan Ouellette, Jen Purcell, Doug Slaybaugh, and Ke-Wen Wang gave moral support and generous feedback during the long process. Others in the Saint Michael's community who deserve special recognition are students in my upper-level seminars who read and critiqued chapter drafts, Traci Griffith, Denise Groll, Lorrie Smith, Karen Talentino, Jeff Trumbower, and Jane Veins. This is by no means an exhaustive list, and I thank the community for their support.

Special recognition goes to my student helper, Monica McClure, and my daughter, Sarah Voigt, who saved me an inordinate amount of time with their data and bibliographic work. Soror Pam White was an amazing copyeditor. Thank you for the enormous amount of time and energy you put into reading and editing. You've truly got my back. And a huge thanks to Emily Magowan who read drafts and offered much needed support.

Encouragement from my friends was integral to this process. Rough patches were assuaged by Uzi Baram, my #1 Janine Jones Smith, Sundae Knight, the Magowans, Chavella Pittman, Amy Reid, Mary Tesch Scobey, Raijean Watkins, and Daria Young Neal. Friends named and un-named please know how much your love and support means to me.

The support of family has been critical to the book's completion. A variety of cousins and other assorted relatives serve as my personal cheering squad, always giving me confidence that this project would eventually find its completion. My parents urged me on in every endeavor. They taught me to love to read, to aspire to explore, and to want to know more about the lessons the past can teach us. And I hold a special place in my heart for my best friend Tim. He was always there carrying my bags to research locations, sharing his excellent editing skills, offering words of encouragement when the project seemed too far from completion, and is beyond pleased that I am finally finished with this seemingly endless "project."

Map of the Atlantic World

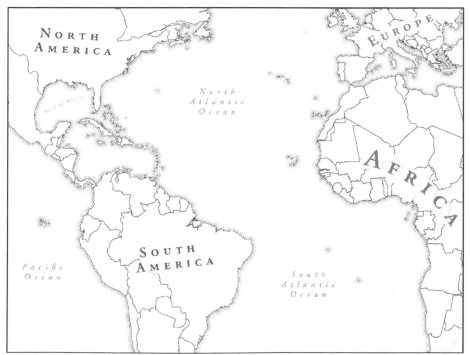

Source: Map drawn by the Cartographic Laboratory, Department of Geography, University of Wisconsin

Chapter One

"People of Different Shades": An Examination of the Nineteenth-Century Population of Puerto Rico

A Contemporary View of the Island

On the way to Mexico in 1822, U.S. diplomat Joel Poinsett's ship made a supply stop in Puerto Rico.[1] Poinsett spent four days on the island making diplomatic visits and obtaining food supplies for the ship. On one foray into the countryside to collect fresh meat and vegetables, he observed that

> In the course of this ride, I met two whites only, but a great many people of different shades of colour ... If they were surprised at our appearance, I was equally so to see such crowds of men, women and children ...[2]

Who were these "great many people of different shades of colour," and why were they so remarkable to this visitor? Poinsett and other North American and European visitors were continually confounded by this island where "the greater part of the free inhabitants are coloured persons," where the "laws know no difference between the white ... and the coloured person,"[3] and where "whites, mulattoes, free people of colour, and slaves, are to be seen promiscuously mingled, without any distinction of place."[4]

Ten years after Poinsett's visit, another account was written by George Flinter, a British national in the service of the Spanish government.[5] Flinter was astounded that "there are more free coloureds here in Puerto Rico than there are on all the French and British islands combined,"[6] and that the "free black and the slave work together in the same field with the white man."[7]

Flinter was often perplexed by encounters on his journey through Puerto Rico. He was hosted by Puerto Rico's elite, which he soon discovered was not synonymous with white. He noted that

> people of all colours and classes are mingled together without any distinction, whose dispositions and interests often clash, among whom private piques exist, and whom injuries, supposed or real might prompt revenge, and yet not one outrage committed, not one insult offered.[8]

Like Poinsett before him, Flinter's journey led him through a land full of a "strange mixture of colours and classes," and he found "everywhere a hearty welcome, good offices, and benevolent feelings."[9] Flinter was unsure what to make of the manner in which the races interacted on a daily basis. His journals describe a land where white and black mixed together in such daily routines as labor, religion, and marriage. Perhaps it was this very reality Flinter, Poinsett, and others feared. What they perceived as indiscriminate mingling between the races must have appeared startling to a white South Carolinian and a British national accustomed to very different social interaction between the races.

The Conceptualization of Race in Colonial Puerto Rico, 1800–1850 examines the social history concerning the social and demographic structure of early nineteenth-century Puerto Rican free people of color. In their studies of nineteenth-century island life, authors Jay Kinsbruner and Francisco Scarano argued that it is difficult to know anything certain about Puerto Rico's social and economic stratification at this current stage in the scholarship.[10] One certainty is that during the first half of the nineteenth century, free people of color constituted over 40 percent of the island's population. During the same period, the white population hovered around 45 percent and the slave population made up the other 15 percent.

Scholars have only recently delved into issues concerning Puerto Rico's nineteenth-century class and social structure. Part of the difficulty stems from the small number of detailed studies about the country's society during this time period.

This study on the country's population of free people of color will provide a broader profile of Puerto Rico's class and social structure. The study combines the broader historiography of Latin American social history with various studies of Puerto Rican urban and rural centers.

Brief History of the Island

The Caribbean country described by Poinsett and Flinter is the smallest, easternmost island of the Greater Antilles. Europeans discovered Puerto Rico on November 19, 1493 during the second voyage of Christopher Columbus. Boriquén, as the local Taíno inhabitants called the island, was now known as the island of San Juan Bautista.[11] The Spanish established a permanent foothold in 1508 under the island's first governor, Juan Ponce de León. A permanent capital city was established on an islet at the entrance of a large bay on one of the finest natural harbors in the Caribbean. As the Spanish Empire in the New World continued to grow, Puerto Rico's primary significance was its strategic location in the eastern Caribbean.[12]

Despite the beautiful harbor and key location, Puerto Rico was a backwater of the Spanish Empire for most of its history. The little colony managed to support a small population of traders, soldiers, government officials, farmers, and cattle herders. Most of its industry was geared toward servicing the garrisons stationed on the island. The capital city, San Juan de Puerto Rico, was the island's main shipping harbor and served as a supply station for ships bound to various ports in the Caribbean, Latin America, and North America. The verdant rolling hills and cooling trade wind breezes made the northern part of the island lush and easily cultivatable. The island itself, 100 miles wide and 30 miles long, was rimmed by mangrove forests that provided for bounteous fishing and offered shelter to contraband ships for smuggling activities.

During the eighteenth century, the Caribbean region emerged as the center of an ever-increasing international trade. The British had succeeded in establishing sugar production on some of their islands in the Lesser Antilles, and trade between them and British colonies in North America became more prominent. Tropical products from Caribbean islands found their way into North American markets in exchange for manufactured goods. The French colony of San Domingue (modern-day Haiti) became one of the world's leading producers of sugar, and the Danish transformed the island of Saint Thomas into a thriving free port. Due to restrictive trade policies mandated from Spain, Puerto Ricans supported a contraband trade that provided almost the only outlet for the island's products. The illegal trade offered a source of much needed goods, including slaves. Practically the entire island's economy in the eighteenth century was based on contraband.[13]

The population of the island was comprised of a mixture of Europeans, Africans, and remnants of the indigenous Taíno peoples. Though the first Africans came to Puerto Rico with the initial Spanish settlers, the decimation of the native Taíno peoples made the introduction of a new African labor force appealing by the middle of the sixteenth century. It was not until the early nineteenth century that the slave labor system began to evolve into one of the island's major institutions.

The population of Puerto Rico remained small throughout its early history. In 1673, there were 820 whites, 304 free mulattoes, and 667 slaves, so subsistence farming and day labor became important to island inhabitants.[14] In 1765, Father Pierre Ledrú lamented to Spanish officials that "pure whites without any outside mixture of the blood are very rare [in Puerto Rico]." Another visiting clergyman noted, "there were very few white families without any mixture of the all the bad races."[15] Accounts by European and North American travelers remarked at how difficult it was to distinguish between black and white in the cities because of the mixture of the races. By 1800, Puerto Rico was known for its unusually large population of free peoples of mixed heritage.

Throughout the nineteenth century, the majority of the people of African descent residing on the island were free. Only a minority among them had ever been enslaved. Puerto Rico's startling demographic and social situation made it unique in the Caribbean context. Specifically, the Puerto Rican slave population never rose above 16 percent, yet the population of free people of color remained over 40 percent during the first half of the nineteenth century. The uniqueness of Puerto Rican social demography was highlighted as the sugar boom increased. No other country in the Caribbean sustained such a high number of free people of color during the time of slavery.

Color Structure of the Early Nineteenth Century

Labels have characterized groups of people for centuries. The encounters between Europeans, Africans, and indigenous peoples in the New World was no exception. In the Spanish Americas, color, birth place, ancestry, and religion all provided ways of classifying groups of people. A myriad of historical, social, and migrational circumstances led to geographical variations on the lexicon of color.

To assist in the understanding of early nineteenth century Puerto Rican social structure, one must understand the basic concepts of color as they were in that region during that time period. In the early nineteenth-century there were three major color classifications for Puerto Rico's non-enslaved population. They included *blanco*, *pardo* or *moreno*, and *negro*. *Blanco* refers to Europeans and their white descendants who were born in the New World. *Pardo* and *moreno* include persons of mixed European and African heritage. *Pardo* was used if the person's phenotypical appearance was more European and *moreno* if it was more African. *Negro* was used for persons of African descent with little or no European mixture. Puerto Rico was quite different from other Hispanic countries in the Western Hemisphere because of its limited vocabulary for people of color. Unlike other slave societies where a litany of color classification placed people of color in a highly stratified system, Puerto Rico never seemed to utilize a rigid color code.[16]

For the purpose of this study, the terms *blanco* and *negro* will be replaced by white and black respectively. The term *pardo* will continue to be used for those Puerto Ricans who are classified as such. The reasoning is that this is a unique derivation by which Puerto Ricans described themselves in the early nineteenth century.[17] The term used most frequently to encompass all people of African descent who were legally free was *gente de color*, which translates to "people of color." The translated term will be used to combine both *pardo* and black free people.

New terms and word combinations for multiracial peoples developed from the mixture of people from around the globe. Euphemisms for blacks and people of mixed race from the colonial Spanish period included *mulato* for African/European, *mestizo* for Indian/European mix, and *gente de color* to encompass persons of mixed heritage. Depending on what shade of brown a person was and where they lived, they could be termed a *pardo*, a *moreno*, a *mulato*, or a wide variety of other names. The definition of each of these, and countless other words used to describe people of African and Native American descent, varied by country and region. If *pardo* in most places meant a more European phenotype within the broad *mulato* grouping, in other places it could mean the opposite.

Among Spanish speakers in the Americas, the terminology and the time of introduction of individual terms varied greatly from one country to another. The racial classification had legal implications, which were used for census and tax purposes. There was no consensus on the meaning of racial categories throughout the Americas, and there were even greater problems of classifying individuals in their proper racial category. Racial terms had genealogical implications requiring precise knowledge of an individual's ancestry on both sides, at a minimum, for two generations. In the Americas, the reality was that high rates of illegitimacy, concealment of parentage, lack of well-defined surnames, and other factors rendered elaborate family trees inaccurate. In Puerto Rico, individuals were often assigned racial classification based mainly according to the arbitrary human perception of how they looked and acted within the community structure. Color, therefore, is a central issue in this study. How documents defined color and how individuals defined themselves help to illustrate the nature of race relations on this particular Caribbean island during the late eighteenth and early nineteenth centuries.

The Puerto Rican Free Person of Color before 1800

The beginnings of the population of free people of color in Puerto Rico can be found in the sexual unions between whites and enslaved or free blacks. These unions were usually considered illegitimate by the church and the Spanish government, although many were cases of cohabitation and consensual relationships. Before 1800, religious marriages were difficult for the majority of the free population of Puerto Rico, regardless of color. The reason for the limited number of sanctioned unions had its roots in the colonial conditions of life. Poverty and lack of roads prevented inhabitants from using the services of the extremely small number of clergy who serviced the island. The majority of the population, including the priests, came to accept cohabitation as natural. These "marriages," though not canonically legal, were socially valid and accepted.

A circular dating from 1700 claims that Puerto Rico had 20,000 inhabitants, but unfortunately for the historian in the twenty-first century, it does not make a distinction as to their racial classification. By 1759, the total island population, including slaves, had risen to 37,923 individuals. In the year 1765, Puerto Rico had 44,883 inhabitants of whom 89 percent were free people, and 11 percent were slaves.[18] More consistent and comprehensive census records began in 1777, but before that time, regrettably, census efforts were sporadic and often incomplete.

After 1777, the population inventory was divided into one section each for *blancos, pardos libres, negros libres, mulatos esclavos, negros esclavos,* and a general total. These sections were then further divided into the categories of man, woman, boy, and girl. These classifications continued with minimal modification until slavery was abolished in 1872.

This new classification system for the census takers illustrated how free people of color were increasing as a percentage of the population total. After 1777, it became easier to track the significance of this important group of people and better gauge their impact on Puerto Rican society.

Puerto Rican Free People of Color

During the nineteenth century, the population of free people of color grew considerably. Previous studies have not shown if this growth was accompanied by changes in the social and economic roles within Puerto Rican society. The majority of authors concentrated on the slave society and the slave population. They failed to consider the major role of free people of color as a societal element.

Puerto Rican free people of color occupied an economic position that traditionally was closed to those of their class in other regions of the Caribbean. The large numbers of free people of color in Puerto Rico allowed them a unique position in the society. Due to their distinctive position, they managed to obtain better rights and to change the prevailing perception regarding people of African descent.

Locating this study outside of the walled city of San Juan geographically and economically separates the free person of color in an urban zone from the free person of color of the rural zone. The intent is to visualize the distinct characteristics that distinguish the free person of color in demographic, economic, and social terms. The aforementioned was accomplished by investigating the social and economic participation of free people of color in non-metropolitan Puerto Rico and the social–racial relations that characterized non-urban Puerto Rican society. This study will examine the mechanics of control and repression that were utilized to maintain free people of color in a position of inferiority. Specific documentation concerning the impact of global and regional events, which helped to thwart the repressive measures, will also be investigated. While it was difficult, there still remained the possibility that free people of color could ascend in Puerto Rico's social hierarchy. For instance, the church was a main force in attempts to control the sexual conduct of the community and to regulate social and sexual relationships among its constituents, but free people of color in Puerto Rico utilized ecclesiastical records to manipulate their space within the island society. *The Conceptualization of Race in Colonial Puerto Rico* explores how free people of color used these forces to their benefit.

Understanding the social and demographic issues confronting people of color throughout the island depends on a variety of sources. The census permits the compilation of information such as age, civil state, place of origin, and occupation. While no complete census exists of the entire island prior to 1850, available records serve to establish distinctions between groups that comprise the population. The extant census records help us to better understand various demographics such as phenotype, age, and gender. They also help us to see how Puerto Ricans perceived themselves and how they were categorized by government officials.

Many of the census materials contain errors that have little relevance to the study, but they still must be mentioned. For example, on occasion, the age of a person on an 1823 census may not correlate with the age of the same person on an 1833 census. In other records the name might appear without a last name, though a previous records contained a last name. These occasional small errors in the records do not alter the final data significantly, but the deficiencies in the sources should be noted.

Nineteenth-century Puerto Rico was a unique Caribbean society where the numbers of free people of color greatly outnumbered the slave population and nearly equaled the white population. The majority of people of African descent living on the island were free. No other country in the Caribbean sustained such a large community of free people of color. Further chapters will illuminate the roles played by these free people of color in early nineteenth-century Puerto Rican class and social structure.

Notes

1. Joel Poinsett was South Carolina's Congressional Representative from 1821–1825. He was named as the first U.S. Foreign Minister to Mexico from 1825–1829 and later served as Secretary of War under Van Buren from 1837–1841. For further

reading consult: Charles Lyon Chandler and R. Smith, "The Life of Joel Roberts Poinsett," *Pennsylvania Magazine of History and Biography* (1935): 1–31; Dorothy Martha Parton, *The Diplomatic Career of Joel Roberts Poinsett: A Dissertation...* (Catholic University of America, 1934); Justin Harvey Smith, "Poinsett's career in Mexico," *American Antiquarian Society*, 1914.

2. Joel Roberts Poinsett, *Notes on Mexico Made in the Autumn of 1822, Accompanied by an Historical Sketch of the Revolution and Translations of Official Reports on the Present State of That Country With a Map. By a Citizen of the United States.* 1824 (New York: Praeger, 1969), 8.

3. Poinsett, *Notes on Mexico*, 7.

4. George D. Flinter, *An Account of the Present State of the Island of Puerto Rico. Comprising Numerous Original Facts and Documents Illustrative of the State of Commerce and Agriculture, and of the Condition, Moral and Physical, of the Various Classes of the Population in That Island, as Compared With the Colonies of Other European Powers; Demonstrating the Superiority of the Spanish Slave Code, – the Great Advantages of Free Over Slave Labor, &c.* (London: Longman, Rees, Orme, Brown, Green, and Longman, 1834), 256.

5. A more detailed analysis of Flinter's work will be found later in this work. Flinter, *An Account of the Present State*, 257–82; Francisco A. Scarano, *Sugar and Slavery in Puerto Rico: The Plantation Economy in Ponce, 1800–1850* (Madison: University of Wisconsin Press, 1984), 26–29.

6. Flinter, *An Account of the Present State*, 26.

7. Ibid., 8.

8. Ibid., 68–70.

9. Ibid., 68–9.

10. Jay Kinsbruner, *Not of Pure Blood: The Free People of Color and Racial Prejudice in Nineteenth-Century Puerto Rico* (Durham, NC: Duke University Press, 1996); Scarano, *Sugar and Slavery*, 1984.

11. The town Ciudad de Puerto Rico ("rich port") was founded on San Juan Bay in 1521. Sometime during the 1520s, confusion over the names led to a switch, the island took the name of Puerto Rico and the town became San Juan.

12. By the mid–sixteenth century, the port at Havana, Cuba had eclipsed San Juan in importance. Luis M. Díaz Soler, *Puerto Rico: Desde sus orígenes hasta el cese de la dominación española* (San Juan: Editorial de la Universidad de Puerto Rico), 1994. For information on the Taínos, see chapter 3 of Díaz Soler. For information on the establishment of a Spanish colony on the island, see chapter 4 of Díaz Soler and see Arturo Morales Carrión, *Puerto Rico: A Political and Cultural History* (New York: W. W. Norton & Company, 1983).

13. Spain attempted to control the contraband trade by employing privateers to patrol the waters around Puerto Rico. Puerto Rican privateers often combined plundering and trading with their defensive tasks. One of the island's most famous

privateers was a mulatto named Miguel Henríquez, a former shoemaker. He became known throughout the Caribbean for his service to the Spanish Crown. In July 1713, Henríquez helped defend the island from a British invasion. He again helped defend the island from the English by leading a force of black lancers from the town of Cangrejos to assist the Spanish navy. Philip V named him Captain of the Sea and War and Provider of the Corsairs of Puerto Rico. He also bestowed on him the title of Knight of the Royal Image. Centro de Investigaciones Históricas [hereafter CIH], Colección Arthur Schomburg, micropeliculas, Reel 7, Box 11; Díaz Soler, *Desde sus orígenes*, 246.

14. The numbers in 1673 were so small (1,791 inhabitants—inclusive of slaves) that the governor of the island requested Spain to send a shipment of white people to the island to augment the population. Salvador Brau, *Historia de Puerto Rico.* Primera edición 1904 (San Juan, PR: Editorial Coqui, 1966), 70–2.

15. Andre Pierre Ledrú, *Viaje a la isla de Puerto Rico en el año 1797 de orden de su gobierno y bajo la dirección del Capitán N. Baudin* (Puerto Rico: Imprenta Militar de J. Gonzalez, 1863), 259.

16. By the 1838 census, the term *pardo* had officially replaced the term *mulato* and was usually combined with the *moreno* category on the majority of census forms.

17. The term *pardo* can be found in other Spanish-speaking regions and most often refers to a person of African descent with light skin or dark skin depending on the region. I have found no other country that uses it as a distinct "catch-all" classification in the manner of Puerto Rico.

18. Archivo General de Puerto Rico [hereafter AGPR], Fondo Gobernadores Españoles de Puerto Rico [hereafter FGEPR], Political and Civil Affairs. Censo y Riqueza. 1801–1820.

Chapter Two

A Changing World: The Atlantic World through the Eyes of Free People of Color

Throughout the Atlantic World, the tumultuous generations between 1780 and 1850 experienced civil wars, political intrigue, and social change as the order of the day. The Industrial Revolution gained momentum, changing European and American economic emphasis from rural and agricultural to urban and manufacturing. Inspired self-proclaimed patriots fought for democratic ideals, toppled monarchies, and changed empires. Societies in ferment challenged cultural norms and reassessed racial and economic caste systems. The realignment opened doors for the expansion of new nations, new governments, and new ideologies. Social and political boundaries were redefined, which caused loyalties to shift in a changing environment.

Puerto Rico was not immune from these broad upheavals. Comprehension of specific world events is necessary to clearly understand the universe in which the people of Puerto Rico lived. This chapter provides a brief overview of explicit world rebellions and revolutions that had serious political and social implications that impacted the entire globe. Against this background, it explores important political documents that were relevant to free people of color in early nineteenth-century

Puerto Rico. Placing Puerto Rico in a broader Atlantic, Caribbean, and colonial context will assist in exploring, more fully, the society and culture in which an unusually large population of free people of color survived and at times even thrived.

Revolutions, Rebellions, and Wars

The structure of the Western world was fundamentally changed due to the revolutions and rebellions during the late eighteenth and early nineteenth centuries. French royalists fought a losing battle against a tyrannical Napoleon. The impertinent United States of America claimed its independence from Britain. Upstart Spanish colonies rose in rebellion against Spain. Infuriated Caribbean slaves violently revolted against their white masters. The impact of the aforementioned tumultuous global events had a real and varied impact upon the island colony of Puerto Rico. Certain occurrences directly shook the society's foundation while other affairs contributed to smaller and more indirect marks in the social, economic, and cultural life of the island. Each global event, in its own way, changed the fabric of the world in which Puerto Rico's free people of color lived and died.

Caribbean Territorial Wars

Throughout the history of European domination in the Caribbean region, the Caribbean islands were the stage for dramatic scenes of warfare and diplomatic manipulations. The islands served as pawns in European war games passing back and forth between powers, often with violent consequences for the island's inhabitants.

One example of this turmoil is the great colonial assets France held in the Caribbean at the close of the eighteenth century. Napoleon Bonaparte correctly assumed that without revenue from his profitable Caribbean sugar islands, France could not pay for the costly wars occurring on European soil. Throughout the eighteenth century, Napoleon and his predecessors did not dare leave their Caribbean islands undefended and vulnerable to Spanish, British, or other European fortune hunters. French officials had to contend continually with opportunistic colonial rivals who were determined to strip France of her territorial wealth.

Great Britain, the powerful naval empire, was France's main enemy during the late eighteenth and early nineteenth centuries. The intense rivalry between the empires caused both sides to make drastic miscalculations in their tactics. The French governments underestimated the destructive forces let loose by untimely declarations of equality to free people of color and emancipation of slaves during the revolutionary fervor of the late 1700s.[1] France grievously underestimated British naval superiority; moreover, British strategists overestimated the support they would receive from royalist French planters on expropriated islands. Their soldiers were not prepared for the French use of revolutionary battle cries that rallied people, military and civilian alike, to challenge social and economic inequities. In short, French insurgents could make revolutions but not always control them; the British military could capture islands but not always hold them.

Both nations sent fleets to the Caribbean in 1793. The British captured Martinique, Guadeloupe, Saint Lucia, and Tobago in 1794 and Trinidad in 1797.[2] Four years later, Great Britain stood as the main force in the Caribbean, the territorial winner in a major turn-of-the-century political upheaval. By 1801, the French were confined mainly to Guadeloupe and the Spaniards to Cuba and Puerto Rico, while Hispañola was controlled by the armies of General Toussaint L'Ouverture.

In a crazy political twist, the 1802 Treaty of Amiens returned all of Britain's latest conquests to their pre-war owners. Napoleon Bonaparte used this brief interlude from fighting to attempt to establish firm control over the French islands as well as his North American possessions. A renewal of hostilities between the European powers in 1803 allowed Britain to regain all of the territory she had lost before the Treaty of Amiens.[3] Napoleon decided to balance his losses after being overwhelmed with territorial losses in Europe and the devastating casualties within his troops, due to disease and warfare in Europe and the Americas. Mostly due to the costly and effective war waged by the former slaves of San Domingue, Napoleon negotiated the sale of over 800,000 square miles of French territory in North America to the fledgling United States and deemed the Caribbean situation hopeless.[4] By the winter of 1803, all that remained of France's once-glorious American empire were Guadeloupe, Martinique, and a small strip of land at the top of South America.

For Great Britain, animosities with its former North American colonies led to blockades of American and Caribbean ports by the British navy in the 1770s. For Spanish officials in Puerto Rico, the blockades created an economic dilemma as they deliberated how to balance conflicting interests regarding Great Britain and the U.S. without losing valuable trading partners in the region. Changes were transpiring in Spanish South America due to political turmoil within the Spanish government and the shift in the balance of power between France and Britain. The subsequent relaxation of trade restrictions throughout Spanish America caused favorable market and trade conditions for Puerto Rico. The colony benefitted financially from these lax trade arrangements since her products were now able to reach a wider market. In the first decades of the nineteenth century, the demand for the coffee, rum, and the delicate lace produced on the island increased dramatically. This, in turn, helped to stimulate the island's economy and benefitted the colony.

The major result of the political and military turmoil within the Caribbean was the realignment of territory and displacement of people throughout the region. Puerto Rico benefitted from upheavals most directly through the influx of immigrants. French immigrants left an indelible mark on Puerto Rico's history. They came from the French islands of Guadeloupe, Martinique, and the former San Domingue. Those who came, both black and white, were industrious and highly skilled. Many were accomplished tradesmen or planters whose expertise helped propel Puerto Rico's agricultural economy into a new era. Planters, influenced by new ideas from Europe and the United States, built coffee plantations from scratch and improved outdated sugar mills to standards as yet untested on the island.[5]

Tailors, seamstresses, shoemakers, and hairdressers brought couture skills from Martinique, the "Paris of the West," to a rising merchant and planter class that now had money to spend. During the early nineteenth century, merchants from San Domingue and Martinique brought trade skills and enticed clients to an island whose sugar, coffee, and other agricultural products were beginning to gain recognition in the world market.

The ideology of brotherhood and rights of man were essential concepts gleaned from the French Revolution.[6] The spark of liberty, the chance to throw off the tyranny of the monarchy and determine the destiny of their own country were appealing concepts for Puerto Ricans, as they were for citizens of other countries. The parlors and drawing rooms of influential Puerto Ricans echoed the same liberating sentiments as those in Venezuela, Martinique, or Boston. While the wheels of democracy turned slowly in Puerto Rico (sometimes one might even feel they moved in reverse) headway was being made for self-determination. Free people of color figured prominently in the political movements of the nineteenth century.[7]

Dissatisfaction in the Spanish Colonies

During the long colonial period, the ideology of the peoples of Spanish America changed significantly. A feeling of social equality among colonials born in the New World replaced the feeling of social inferiority that had prevailed earlier when American-born colonists confronted those born on the Iberian Peninsula. A group consciousness matured into feelings of nationalism, placing high value on the land of one's birth and dedicating political and social energy to the *patria* (homeland).

Changing attitudes were two-fold. First, those in the Spanish colonies developed a greater appreciation and pride regarding the regions where they were born and raised. Secondly, there arose a fuller understanding that their own interests could be better served if they, and not distant monarchs, made fundamental economic and political decisions. Greater self-awareness intensified the Spanish colonial resentment of the authority, control, and direction of faraway government.

Concentrating earnestly on themselves and their surroundings, the colonials searched for new ways to improve their condition.

Inspired by the North American example and encouraged by the changes wrought by Haitian patriots, Spanish colonies declared their independence in an effort to embrace their potential and launch into a new era. Ideas emanating from the newly formed United States—that nation's declaration and struggle for independence, and the resulting republic that was formed—fascinated Latin American intellectuals. Radical Haitian ideals of freedom and equality, along with French ideals of brotherhood and republican ideals of government, inspired the colonial elite to challenge Spanish control.

Colonists sensed that Spain was no longer the power it had once been. For Spain, the first decade of the nineteenth century was a period of political turmoil and military disasters, which eventually brought about the collapse of its American empire. The suspension of trade and the ever increasing burden of war brought Spain to an economic and political crisis. This crisis was only worsened by governmental attempts to raise revenues to finance the war. Government expropriation of ecclesiastical properties displeased the powerful Catholic Church. Large quantities of paper currency fed inflation and increased popular dissent. Opposition raged against the Crown Prince and in 1808, faced with open rebellion and popular rioting, Charles IV abdicated to allow his son to assume the throne as Ferdinand VII. At the same time, Napoleon Bonaparte's armies marched into the Iberian Peninsula. Ferdinand became Napoleon's prisoner, Napoleon's brother Joseph Bonaparte was declared king of Spain, and Spain's major cities were occupied by French troops. Spanish resistance to the occupation led to the coexistence of two governments in Spain. The government of the French invaders was led by King Joseph I, while the Spanish government continued to operate in three parts: the Junta Central, the Regency, and the Cortes. The effect this had on the American colonies was a movement toward independence. What began under the guise of preserving Ferdinand VII's rights later became open rebellion against Spanish rule.[8] The unsettled state of the Spanish colonies and the Napoleonic intrusion into Iberia forced Spain to give her colonies unprecedented access to trade with foreigners, which prompted an increase in extra-legal trade throughout Spanish America. As an example, British exports to Spanish Cuba more than tripled during the two years of the war. The British colonies of Jamaica and Trinidad profited greatly from the increase of Latin American trade between 1808 and 1815.

Since the 1550s, the official trade policy of the Crown had given exclusive trading rights in the Spanish colonies to Spanish ships and strictly channeled money, goods, and treasures through officially sanctioned ports. In order to maintain any semblance of an economy on the island, Puerto Rican government officials turned a blind eye to, or shared in the revenue of, a long history of contraband trade. Ships from Spain, carrying much-needed supplies to the islanders, were few and far between. Spanish merchants feared losing their ships to the pirates who utilized Puerto Rico's plentiful mangrove inlets and well-concealed harbors to intercept legitimate ships. The colony's relative lack of wealth deterred merchants from risking their ships for small gain. On the island, exporters resisted the Crown's decree that all commerce be shipped exclusively through San Juan's harbor. High duties, excessive shipping costs, and a poor transportation infrastructure on the island added to the difficulty of exclusively trading out of San Juan.

Unable to trade legally through San Juan, savvy Puerto Rican merchants turned very early to contraband trade with Spain's rivals. By the mid–seventeenth century, the island supported a thriving illegal trade that the Crown repeatedly tried to restrain. Their attempts always met with failure. Spain was never able to sufficiently satisfy the needs of its Puerto Rican colonists. Both Puerto Ricans and government officials stationed on the island found the illicit trade to be the lifeline of the colony. By the nineteenth century, contraband trade was an integral part of the island economy. The turmoil in Spain in the early 1800s allowed for some relaxation in trade policies; however, when the Crown regained control and tried to reassert limited trade restrictions, her American colonies (just Puerto Rico and Cuba by 1840) balked at the renewed restraints.

The outbreak of war between Great Britain and the United States led to blockades of North American ports by the British navy. Great Britain imposed an embargo on merchant ships from the United States between 1807 and 1809, and again in 1815. Combined with lax Spanish enforcement, this had the effect of temporarily removing a vigorous competitor from the Caribbean, thus allowing Puerto Rico and other Spanish colonies to trade directly with the Dutch, British, and French colonies throughout the Caribbean.[9]

Merchandise was not the only thing moving around the Caribbean in this era. Puerto Rico was influenced by an influx of immigrants to its shores. Immigrants fleeing civil strife in Europe and in the Americas flowed into Puerto Rico, both legally and illegally. Some were fortunate enough to bring money and prestige with them, but many were destitute and hoped for a better life and a new beginning on the small island. The fervor of war and independence was not lost on these new immigrants, and they passed their experience with revolutionary ideas and tactics on to their new neighbors. Spain, trying not to antagonize one of its two remaining loyal colonies in the Americas, allowed the island government latitude in terms of political and mercantile freedoms, enacting economic as well as social reforms.[10] The 1815 *Cédula de Gracias al Sacar* (explained later in this chapter) was a direct result of Spanish desires to appease supporters in Puerto Rico. For the most part, the benefit for Puerto Rico was the new, if minimal, allowance for island self-determination. It also opened trade that, in turn, stimulated growth in the economy by building demand for Puerto Rican coffee and sugar products, especially in the nearby North American market.[11] For free people of color, this opened a market niche that they could capitalize and exploit for social and economic gain.

The Haitian Revolution

By far the most frightening rebellion in the Western Hemisphere took place on the French Caribbean island of San Domingue between 1795 and 1804. Resulting in the second independent nation in the Americas, the first and only successful slave rebellion put fear in the hearts and minds of countries whose economies, cultures, and social orders depended on the constructs of slavery. Social and political legislation initiated throughout the Americas after this unprecedented event reflected how vulnerable the white minority felt among their black majority. Increasing numbers of rebellions, and the ferocious measures used to quell them, demonstrated just how much of an impact the Haitian event had on populations throughout the region. Stringent countermeasures in the form of codes, legislation, or white-on-black violence followed the fear of black insurgency.

The Haitian Revolution translated the battle cries of a white European revolution into black Caribbean action. The reaction of enslaved black workers to the harshness of plantation owners generated an explosion of internal forces. Haiti demonstrated to people of African descent throughout the Atlantic World how the much-practiced cries of liberty, fraternity, and equality could be used to destroy the institution of slavery. News of the revolution in San Domingue sparked numerous other rebellions, revolts, and civil unrest throughout the region.[12] The majority of these uprisings were as significantly African in character as the revolt in Haiti.

Slaveowners all over the Atlantic World were well aware of the dangers of a "spirit of subversion"—and had been so even before the unrest in San Domingue. In San Domingue itself, the slaveowners utilized their own "spirit of subversion" against their French colonizers in the spirit of French revolutionary ideals by sending delegates to the 1789 meeting of the Estates-General. In 1791, white slave owners from the French Caribbean colonies openly defied the very French government they would soon turn to for support and safety by demanding and receiving a large degree of local autonomy from the Paris National Assembly. The Assembly then chose to extend the vote to *all* free persons, including free people of color. In San Domingue, white planters' demand for a repeal of the law led to open defiance of the French government and a power struggle with free people of color within the colony. Black slaves utilized this divisive moment as an opportunity to liberate themselves.[13]

The balance of power in the Caribbean, and in Europe itself, was threatened by the Haitian revolt. Napoleon was successful in regaining control of Martinique and Guadeloupe, returning them to their former status as slaveholding sugar colonies under French control. Yet he failed in his attempts to quell the unrest in the former "Pearl of the Antilles." The British and the Spanish, in a quest to control an important strategic location within the Caribbean, were also unsuccessful in their attempts to wrest control from the former slaves of San Domingue. In January 1804, Haiti emerged from the fray as the second independent nation in the Western Hemisphere. It was a beacon of hope for the hemisphere's black enslaved millions; however, Haiti was also a chilling reminder for the hemisphere's plantation owners.

Puerto Rico benefitted from the influx of immigrants during and after the hostilities. The western part of Puerto Rico still bears the influences of this mostly prosperous group of immigrants, both white and free people of color, in its architecture and agricultural emphasis. Rich planters brought the latest technology and their knowledge of sugar production to the Puerto Rican countryside and helped spur an economic boom.

Along with its many benefits, the Haitian Revolution also brought a growing fear of slave revolts to Puerto Rican society. Fear was compounded in part due to the rising number of slaves on the island. Knowledge of increasing slave uprisings throughout the Caribbean after the conclusion of the Haitian Revolution was also a concern. Major slave conspiracies were uncovered on the island in 1821 and 1823. Puerto Rican authorities were quick to blame them on subterfuge and clandestine activity from Haiti rather than on the inhumane system of slavery on the island that produced the conspiracies.[14]

In 1826, the Puerto Rican government enacted a new slave code, the *Reglamento de los Esclavos* ("Slave Regulations"). Its intention was to intimidate the slaves into submission by subjecting them to much harsher conditions than were already in place on the island.[15] The *Reglamento* was a direct result of the fears of slave conspiracy and revolt that gripped Puerto Rico, the Caribbean, and the Atlantic World.[16]

The 1822 Haitian troops, under the command of President Jean-Pierre Boyer, invaded the western side of Hispañola in the name of liberating slaves, unifying the people of African descent, and claiming territory for Haiti.[17] Puerto Rican officials and Spanish officials must have felt some anxiety about the ease by which the Haitians could cross the Mona Passage, a distance of only eighty miles at its closest point from eastern Hispañola to Puerto Rico's western coast.[18]

For Puerto Rico's free colored population, the threats of slave rebellions and of Haitian domination were equally terrorizing. Many new immigrants fled the former French colony in search of a more stable and accommodating environment. The strict 1826 regulations governing Puerto Rican slaves were not applied to the free colored population of the island. In this important separation, the new laws were unlike similar regulations in other Caribbean slave-based societies, including the Spanish colony of Cuba.[19]

Climate in Early Nineteenth-Century Puerto Rico

Free people of African descent in Puerto Rico, similar to their counterparts throughout the Atlantic World, dealt with many legal issues related to social equality. These issues are best examined by looking closely at several significant and far-reaching laws. Three government documents were essential to the early nineteenth-century history of free people of color in Puerto Rico. The 1812 Constitution of Cádiz clarified the political position of free people of color in the Spanish colonies. The 1815 *Cédula de Gracias al Sacar* explicitly allowed for the inclusion of free people of color in its immigration campaign. The 1848 *Bando Contra la Raza Africana*, even in its short existence, was a reminder of the tenuous and often capriciously-granted rights free people of color held within Puerto Rico.

1812 Constitution of Cádiz

The 1812 Constitution of Cádiz was drawn up by the Cortés, the parliamentary governance body in Spain. The delegates of the Spanish

Cortés at Cádiz faced many dilemmas that affected their overseas possessions. Signs of Spain's weakness included her loss of Santo Domingo to France in 1796 and Trinidad to England in 1797, as well as the devastating loss of her navy in the 1805 Battle of Trafalgar.[20] For Puerto Ricans, the new constitution extended basic rights of inviolability of house, person, property, speech, voting, and freedom of work. The island was authorized to have a *diputado* (representative) to be selected by a system of indirect vote at three levels: the parish, the district, and the province.

A major issue before the Spanish Cortés was the question of colonial representation. If people of color were included in determining representation, the colonies would have a greater representation in the Cortés than would Spain. To resolve this issue, Article 22 of the constitution declared that all men born free and residing in Spanish territory were to be considered Spaniards, as were freed slaves. The colored castes, however, were excluded from citizenship, thereby solving the problem of over-representation in the colonies. Article 22 also stated that free people of color could not vote in elections, be counted for the purpose of determining representation in future parliaments, or hold municipal offices.[21]

These laws presented an interesting conundrum for free people of color in Puerto Rico. Many of them were considered socially to be white, yet few had gone through the legal channels to become "whitened." How would they participate in the political forum? What did this mean for them when it came time to vote? Could any of them run for office? The answer must be yes for a select few who had slipped into white society, but a strong no for those who were trapped by the legalities of colonial Spain. Simply put, numerous offices were off limits to those whose ancestry was not white. Some leeway may have been allowed in local offices where community standing and family position could weigh more heavily than Spanish law. When higher colonial positions were sought, however, it was harder to circumvent the necessary documentation and pedigree. No records have been found of free people of color holding the office of *alcalde* (mayor) or *diputado* (representative).[22]

Cédula de Gracias al Sacar

A second important document that affected Puerto Rico's community of free people of color was the *Real Cédula de Gracias al Sacar* of 1815. Ferdinand VII of Spain issued the decree on August 10, 1815 with the goal of promoting the development of Puerto Rico's commerce, industry, and agriculture. The primary aim of the document was to isolate the island from the turmoil in other areas of the empire and to insure the continued loyalty of his Puerto Rican subjects. One major thrust of the decree was to increase Puerto Rico's population, thereby making it more stable and providing greater support for the Crown.

Puerto Rico was suffering from a declining overall population at the turn of the nineteenth century. The trend consisted of the steady decline of the white population while both the free and enslaved colored populations were slowly rising. The Spanish government, searching for ways in which to augment the island's declining population, chose the 1815 *Cédula de Gracias al Sacar* as the answer. This document invited peoples from regions loyal to the Spanish Crown or to the Catholic Church to settle in Puerto Rico, giving them land and tax-exempt status. Free people of color were explicitly included in this invitation, although they only received a third of the benefits white settlers could expect.[23]

The *Cédula* was Spain's attempt to reward the inhabitants of Puerto Rico for their service and loyalty during the early wars of independence by liberalizing trade and stimulating the island's economy.[24] Spain's political maneuver must have had an impact because between 1800 and 1900, Puerto Rico's population exploded from 150,000 to nearly a million. As part of the *Cédula's* policy, migration of both whites and free people of color was encouraged. Each colonist was granted a standard amount of land on which to settle, with an equal amount granted to each member of the household. Seven acres were granted to white colonists and three acres for free *negro* or *pardo* colonists. White colonists, of either sex, who brought slaves with them received additional acres for each slave, equal to one-half their initial allotment. A free person of color who was a head of family was granted the same amount of land that was calculated for the slave of a white settler. Slaves brought by a free person of color entitled him to additional land equal to half that which was calculated for slaves accompanying whites.[25]

The new settlers were granted tax exemption for ten years; thereafter, they were to be taxed yearly one peso per slave. Free people of color were only offered a five-year tax exemption. The tax exemption for both white and free colored was effective at all times except during times of war or in an emergency.

Any settler was allowed to leave the island during the first five years with all his belongings, provided he paid a 10-percent tax on all profits made during the stay.[26] After the initial five-year period, the immigrant and his family could become naturalized citizens. As citizens, they then received a permanent title to their land and could acquire additional property. The new settler could move freely around the island, provided he was granted permission from local authorities. Immigrants were free to establish industries or trade at the end of the five-year period. They could actively engage in maritime and commercial enterprises as well as own warehouses or stores. On a settler's death, his properties would pass to his legal heirs, provided they also settled in Puerto Rico.

Immigrants entering under the *Cédula* included refugees from war-torn nations such as the Dominican Republic, the French islands, Costa Firme (Venezuela), and Haiti. Spanish soldiers and officers often settled in Puerto Rico after their tour of duty ended. Immigrants from Spain, the Canary Islands, and Corsica were also common. The majority of free people of color entering Puerto Rico tended to immigrate from Costa Firme, the French islands, Curaçao, and Haiti. More than 656 foreigners and their families took advantage of the liberal provisions provided in the *Cédula*.[27]

The land allotment to free colored immigrants was more than most countries were offering. Some islands published explicit legislation to keep free people of color from immigrating at all, while others made life socially and economically uncomfortable for free colored settlers once they arrived. Conversely, Puerto Rico made an effort to incorporate loyal free colored immigrants into Puerto Rican society. The overall level of skills found among immigrants of color was high; as a result, the economy benefitted due to their contributions to agriculture and trade.

Some scholars have argued that this document was created to boost the white population of Puerto Rico against the rising colored population.[28] This viewpoint can be challenged considering legislation on other islands and other colonial powers during this era tended to explicitly exclude free people of color from their territories—or severely threatened their freedom and opportunities once they were settled.[29] The very fact that free people of color were included in the language of the *Cédula de Gracias al Sacar* demonstrates that the intent was to augment the total population of a floundering colony by getting as many loyal, able, Catholic bodies as possible onto one of the few remaining strongholds of the Spanish Crown. Free people of color demonstrated loyalty, industriousness, and fortitude. It is true that free people of color were given less than their white counterparts; however, the fact remains that they were specifically included in the language of the legislation.

Bando Contra la Raza Africana

The third important document, appearing a generation after the *Cédula*, was the infamous *Bando Contra la Raza Africana* ("Proclamation against the African Race"). This virulent law was circulated by Governor Juan Prim y Prats at the end of May 1848. Prim was only governor for eight months, but his legacy proved far-reaching. On May 31, 1848, Governor Prim informed the Puerto Rican people of an uprising in Martinique. The French ship *Argus* had just pulled into San Juan's harbor, and its distraught refugees relayed news of chilling events on the French island. The Dutch islands of Saint Croix and Saint Thomas soon sent envoys reporting the uprisings had spread to their territories. Upon learning of the destructive activities of the ex-slaves recently liberated by the French in Martinique and Guadeloupe, he interpreted these stories as evidence of the "ferocious stupidity of the African race."[30] Prim promised these islands he would send troops to help quell the violence. He asked the Puerto Rican people to remain calm and trust their governor, as well as the Spanish army, to maintain the peace in Puerto Rico. Governor Prim was determined to lessen the possibility of similar uprisings in Puerto Rico.[31]

According to the 1848 measure, any crime committed by any person of African descent, be they free or slave, would henceforth be judged by a military court. Any free colored person who used arms against a white person, no matter if justified, would have his right hand cut off. In the event that the white person was wounded, the person of color would be executed by a firing squad. Any person of color who insulted a white by word, maltreatment, or threatening manner of any form, would be tried and sentenced according to the circumstances. If two or more people of color were to fight in the streets or other public places, using only their fists, they would be sentenced to fifteen days of work on public roads or be required to pay a fine of twenty-five pesos. If any of the combatants used a stick or stone, with minor wounds resulting, the penalty would be a month's work on the roads or a fine of fifty pesos. If the wounds were grave, the penalty would be four years' incarceration. In the event that firearms were used, the penalties were more severe, up to and including execution.[32]

The preceding virulent document was short-lived; a new governor, Juan de la Pezuela, rescinded it in November of that same year (1848).[33] Nevertheless, the emotional impact that the aforementioned had on the island's free people of color cannot be determined. How many of the principles in the document were actually applied in the six months before it was rescinded are also in question. Despite the fact that the *Bando* was reversed before being fully implemented, its brief existence gave voice to the deep misgivings some white Puerto Ricans had about their colored neighbors. Ideals that gave rise to the ill-fated law remained, and free people of color constantly had to contend with such circumstances.

Conclusion

Nineteenth-century Puerto Rican society was a product of the various events that changed the world. Global events carried political and social implications that shaped island society. The three political documents discussed in this chapter directly affected the lives of free people of color in Puerto Rico. The documents were a product of their time and shed light on how outside influences contributed to the overall position of the community of free people of color in Puerto Rico.

When considering all of these events, it should not be forgotten that slaves constituted a minute part of the total island population, never exceeding 17 percent. It must be noted that the population of free people of color rivaled the free white population, at times reaching over 48 percent of Puerto Rico's total population. These numbers have no counterpart in Caribbean history, which makes the free people of color of Puerto Rico a unique population to study.

Notes

1. In 1795, the French Republican government became the first European government to emancipate all the slaves in their Empire. Napoleon Bonaparte reversed the ruling and reinstated slavery on his remaining Caribbean islands in 1804. For further exploration of the concept of race in France and its colonies see: Sue Peabody and Tyler Stovall, "Introduction: race, France, histories" in *The color of liberty: Histories of race in France* (Durham, NC: Duke University Press), 2003: 1–7.

2. In Martinique, the British made an effective alliance with French royalists, maintaining both slavery and internal peace. Guadeloupe and Saint Lucia were quickly recaptured by the French. Tobago and Trinidad were wrested from the Spanish dominions. 1797 was a pivotal military year for Puerto Rico, with an attack on the capital city of San Juan by British General Ralph Abercromby. After an easy victory over the Spanish in Trinidad, Abercromby turned his sights on Puerto Rico. In mid-April 1797 his troops attempted to take the capital by an overland route to avoid the fortifications of the imperious fort El Morro and the mercenary French privateers, both of whom were protecting San Juan's harbor. Abercromby failed in his mission and was repelled from the island on April 30. The Spanish government gave special recognition to the island's *mulato* and *pardo* militia who fought valiantly and were a major factor in ousting the British troops. Luis M. Díaz Soler, *Puerto Rico: Desde sus orígenes hasta el cese de la dominación española* (San Juan: Editorial de la Universidad de Puerto Rico, 1994), 288–93; Arturo Morales Carrión, *Puerto Rico: A Political and Cultural History* (New York: W. W. Norton & Company), 1983; J. H. Parry, Philip Sherlock, and Anthony Manigot, *A Short History of the West Indies*, 4th ed. (London: Macmillian, 1989), 100.

3. The Battle of Trafalgar in 1805 established the British as the military powerhouse in the Caribbean. The final treaties in 1815 added Saint Lucia, Tobago, Trinidad, Demerara, Esquibo, and Berbice to British possession and returned Martinique and Guadeloupe to France. Return of those territories was in large part due to England's desire for security much closer to home, as it fended off attacks in Europe. For more information on the military balance of power in this era see: Fred Anderson, *Crucible of War: The Seven Years' War and the Fate of Empire in British North America, 1754–1766.* (New York: Alfred A. Knopf, 2000); Humphrey Metzgen and John Graham, *Caribbean Wars Untold: A Salute to the British West Indies* (Kingston, Jamaica: University of West Indies Press, 2007); Alan Gregor Cobley, *Crossroads of Empire: The Europe-Caribbean Connection, 1492–1992* (Cave Hill, Bridgetown, Barbados: Dept. of History, University of the West Indies, 1994); Carrie Gibson, *Empire's Crossroads: A History of the Caribbean from Columbus to the Present Day* (London: Macmillan, 2014); Matthew Mulcahy, *Hubs of Empire: The Southeastern Lowcountry and British Caribbean* (Baltimore: The Johns Hopkins University Press, 2014); Peter Earle, *The Sack of Panamá: Captain Morgan and the Battle for the Caribbean* (New York: Thomas Dunne Books/St. Martin's Press, 2007); Andrew Jackson O'Shaughnessy, *An Empire Divided: The American Revolution and the British Caribbean* (Philadelphia: University of Pennsylvania Press, 2000); J. H. Parry, Philip Sherlock, and Anthony Manigot, *A Short History of the West Indies*, 4th ed. (London: Macmillan, 1989).

4. The Louisiana Purchase was signed in Paris on April 30, 1803, with Robert Livingston and James Monroe for the U.S. and François Barbé Marbois representing France. The U.S. purchased more than 800,000 square miles of land, an area larger than Great Britain, France, Germany, Italy, Spain, and Portugal combined, for the price of 60 million francs, equal to about $15 million. For roughly four cents an acre, France had sold its North American possession encompassing all or part of fifteen current U.S. states and two current Canadian provinces stretching from the Mississippi River to the Rocky Mountains.

5. For more information on the subject of foreign capital and foreign agricultural expertise in the building of Puerto Rico's sugar and coffee industry see: Laird Bergad, *Coffee and the Growth of Agrarian Capitalism in Nineteenth-Century Puerto Rico* (Princeton: Princeton University Press, 1983), 268–69; Luis M. Díaz Soler, *Puerto Rico: Desde sus orígenes hasta el cese de la dominación española* (San Juan: Editorial de la Universidad de Puerto Rico, 1994), 481–86; Francisco Scarano, *Sugar and Slave in Puerto Rico: The Plantation Economy of Ponce, 1800–1850* (Milwaukee: University of Wisconsin Press, 1984), 161–62.

6. The Grito de Lares, on September 23, 1865, directly traces its ideals and demands to the Declaration of the Rights of Man. Díaz Soler, *Desde sus orígenes*, 578–79; Olga Jimenez de Wagenheim, *Puerto Rico: An Interpretive History from Pre Columbian Times to 1900.* (Princeton: Markus Wiener Publishers, 1998), 8.

7. Dr. José Celso Barbosa (1857–1921), a free man of color from Bayamón, is an example of the importance free people of color had in Puerto Rican politics as the colonial era drew to a close. Barbosa came from a family of free artisans. He studied at the Jesuit Seminary in San Juan (the only secondary institute on the island), and in 1880 graduated from the University of Michigan School of Medicine. During the course of his political career he was a statesman, a senator, a writer, and a journalist. His most significant contribution to the Puerto Rican political scene was as founder of the Puerto Rican Republican party. Barbosa dedicated his life to upholding the basic tenets of social justice and self-governance. For more on Barbosa see: Lídio Cruz Monclova, *Historia de Puerto Rico (siglo XIX)*. 6 vols. (Río Piedras: Editoral Universitaria, 1979); Philip Sterling and Maria Brau, *The Quiet Rebels: Four Puerto Rican Leaders* (New York: Doubleday, 1968), 3–35.

8. For a more in-depth look at this tumultuous era of Spanish political history, consult: Díaz Soler, *Desde sus orígenes*, 358–73 and 406–13; Arturo Morales, *Auge y decadencia de la trata negrera en Puerto Rico, 1820–1860* (San Juan: Centro de Estudios Avanzados de Puerto Rico y el Caribe and the Instituto de Cultura Puertorriqueña, 1978), 82; J. M. Roberts, *A History of Europe* (New York: Allen Lane, 1996), 314–19; Edwin Williamson, *The Penguin History of Latin America* (New York: Penguin, 1992), 214–15.

9. Birgit Sonesson, *La real hacienda en Puerto Rico: Administración, política y grupos de presión 1815–1869* (Madrid: Instituto de Estudios Fiscales & Instituto de Cooperación Iberoamericana, 1990), 74–75.

10. For more information on political and economic reforms see: Laird W. Bergard, *Coffee and the Growth of Agrarian Capitalism in Nineteenth-Century Puerto Rico* (Princeton: Princeton University Press, 1983); Díaz Soler, *Desde sus orígenes*; James Dietz, *Economic History of Puerto Rico* (Princeton: Princeton University Press, 1986); Francisco A. Scarano, *Sugar and Slavery in Puerto Rico: The Plantation Economy in Ponce, 1800–1850* (Madison: University of Wisconsin Press, 1984).

11. For more information on the growth of free trade in Puerto Rico and Cuba see: Kinsbruner, *Not of Pure Blood*; Manuel Moreno Fraginals, Frank Moya Pons, and Stanley Engerman, *Between Slavery and Free Labor: The Spanish Speaking Caribbean in the Nineteenth Century* (Baltimore: The Johns Hopkins University Press, 1985); Andres Ramos Mattei, *Azúcar y esclavitud* (San Juan: Ediciones Huracán, 1982).

12. Uprisings and unrest include, but are not limited to, the Second Maroon War in Jamaica, 1795–1796; slave revolts in Suriname, 1798; Fedon's rebellion in Grenada, 1795–1797; the Second Black Carib War in Saint Vincent, 1795–1796; the "Brigand's War" in Saint Lucia, 1796–1799; the black regimental soldiers' mutinies in Dominica, 1802, and Jamaica, 1808; trouble in Belize and Tobago; and plots and unrest in Dominica 1809 and Barbados 1816. Parry, Sherlock, and Maingot, *A Short History*.

13. For excellent detail on this moment see: C. L. R. James, *The Black Jacobins: Toussaint L'Ouverture and the San Domingo Revolution 1963* (New York: Vintage, 1989), 60–61, 95–96; Carolyn E. Fick, *The Making of Haiti: The Saint Domingue Revolution From Below* (Knoxville: University of Tennessee Press, 1990), 76–82.

14. For more information on the impact of Caribbean slave revolts on Puerto Rico and on slave revolts in Puerto Rico see: Guillermo Baralt, *Esclavos rebeldes: Conspiraciones y sublevaciones de esclavos en Puerto Rico (1795–1873)* (Río Piedras: Ediciones Huracán, 1982); Benjamin Nistal Moret, *Esclavos prófugos y cimarrones: Puerto Rico, 1770–1870* (San Juan: Editorial de la Universidad de Puerto Rico, 1984).

15. A good discussion of this 1826 Regulation and its social and political implications can be found in: Baralt, *Esclavos rebeldes*, 35–52 and 67–72.

16. For more information on the slave code see: Baralt, *Esclavos rebeldes*, Chapter 1; Luis Díaz Soler, *Historia de la esclavitud negra en Puerto Rico* (Río Piedras: Editorial Universitaria, 1981), 213–15; Nistal Moret, *Esclavos prófugos y cimarrones*, 11–15.

17. The "Haitian Domination" lasted until 1844 when rebels from the former Spanish colony of Santo Domingo forced Haitian troops back to the former French side and declared the new nation as the Dominican Republic. For more information on the Haitian Occupation of the Dominican Republic see: Frank Moya Pons, *La Dominación Haitian*, 3rd ed., (Santiago: Universidad Católica Madre y Maestra, 1978), passim; Frank Moya Pons, *Historia colonial de Santo Domingo* (Santiago, Dominican Republic: Universidad Católica Madre y Maestra, 1977), 415–24; Frank Moya Pons, *La dominación haitiana* (Santiago, Dominican Republic: Universidad Católica Madre y Maestra, 1978), 212–14; Frank Moya Pons, *The Dominican Republic: A National History* (Princeton: Markus Wiener Publishers, 1998), Chapter 6.

18. On a clear day, the Samaná Peninsula of the Dominican Republic can be seen across the Mona Passage from many towns on Puerto Rico's northwestern coast.

19. For information on Dutch slave regulation see: N. A. T. Hall, "Slave Laws of the Danish Virgin Islands in the Later Eighteenth Century," in *Comparative Perspectives on Slave in New World Plantation Societies*, eds. Vera Rubin and Arthur Tuden (New York: New York Academy of Sciences, 1977), 174–86.

For information on British slave regulation see: Elsa Goveia, *Slave Society in the British Leeward Islands at the End of the Eighteenth Century* (New Haven: Yale University Press, 1965); Elsa Goveia, *Leeward Islands at the End of the Eighteenth Century* (New Haven: Yale University Press, 1965), Chapter 3; Elsa Goveia, *The West Indian Slave Laws of the Eighteenth Century* (Barbados: Caribbean University Press, 1970), 11–19.

For a good discussion on how slave regulations affected free people of color on the British islands see: Mavis C. Campbell, *The Dynamics of Change in a Slave Society: A Sociopolitical History of the Free Coloreds of Jamaica, 1800–1865* (Rutherford, NJ: Fairleigh Dickinson University Press, 1976), Chapter 2.

For information on Cuban slave regulation see: Arthur Corwin, *Spain and the Abolition of Slave in Cuba, 1817–1886* (Austin: University of Texas Press, 1967); Rebecca J. Scott, *Slave Emancipation in Cuba: The Transition to Free Labor, 1860–1899* (Princeton: Princeton University Press, 1990).

20. Spain had become a satellite of France by the end of the eighteenth century. Her backing of France during the Napoleonic Wars caused Spain to lose its once-powerful navy in a humiliating defeat against Britain's Admiral Horatio Nelson at the Battle of Trafalgar. Díaz Soler, *Desde sus orígenes*, 359–60; Jimenez de Wagenheim, *An Interpretive History*, 105; Williamson, *Penguin History*, 210–14.

21. AGPR, FGEPR, Reales Órdenes 1767–1856, caja 175.

22. Records in Puerto Rico are incomplete, but one telling detail about nineteenth-century Puerto Ricans is when and where they decided to describe a person by the color of his or her skin.

23. AGPR, FGEPR, Reales Órdenes 1767–1856, caja 175.

24. Ibid.

25. Cayetano Coll y Toste, *Boletín Histórico de Puerto Rico* (San Juan: Tipografía Cantero Fernández, 1914–1927), 297–307, articles 10 and 11; Centro de Investigaciones Históricas [CIH], Real Cedula de 1815, Leyes, Decretos, Circulares, etc. para el Gobierno de la Isla de Puerto Rico, 1814–1817 (micropelícula).

26. This clause was modified later so the land would revert back to the state if the recipient left the land and/or the island.

27. AGPR, FGEPR, Emigrados 1815–1837, caja 54; AGPR, FGEPR, Extrangeros, cajas 89–115.

28. AGPR, FGEPR, Reales Ordenes 1767–1856, caja 175; Díaz Soler, *Desde sus orígenes*, 378–94 and 421–24; José Luis González, *Puerto Rico: The Four-Storyed Country and Other Essays* (New York: Markus Wiener, 1993), 35–36; Jimenez de Wagenheim, *An Interpretive History*, 148–50; Kinsbruner, *Not of Pure Blood*, 41–42).

29. See footnote 32 for information regarding restrictions on free people of color and slaves in other Caribbean colonies.

30. CIH, Bando Contra la Raza Africana, Leyes, Decretos, Circulares, etc. para el Gobierno de la Isla de Puerto Rico, 1833–1870, (micropelícula).

31. Coll y Toste, *Boletín Histórico*, 79–91; Díaz Soler, *Desde sus orígenes*, 448.

32. These are the penalties relating to free people of color. Slaves were assigned separate penalties. Slave uprisings, while not frequent, did occur in Puerto Rico. AGPR, FGEPR, Reales Ordenes 1767–1856, caja 175; Luis M. Díaz Soler, *Historia de la esclavitud negra en Puerto Rico* (Río Piedras: Editorial Universitaria, Universidad de Puerto Rico, 1981), 217–21; Coll y Toste, *Boletín Histórico*, 80–85); CIH, Bando Contra la Raza Africana, Leyes, Decretos, Circulares, etc. para el Gobierno de la Isla de Puerto Rico, 1833–1870, (micropelícula).

33. Coll y Toste, *Boletín Histórico*, 89–91. See also: Baralt, *Esclavos Rebeldes*, 127–31.

Chapter Three

Living in Color: Native and Immigrant Free People of Color in Their Communities

Throughout most of the island's history, the majority of Puerto Rico's inhabitants were rural free colored and poor whites, engaged in subsistence agriculture and seeking out a paltry existence in the colonial backwater. In the eighteenth century, Spain refused to see Puerto Rico as anything other than a military outpost, and the island's economy remained underdeveloped. It was not until 1815 that the economic development of Puerto Rico received official support. In that year, King Ferdinand VII issued the *Real Cédula de Gracias al Sacar,* which liberalized trade, offered incentives for immigrants, and opened Puerto Rican ports to legal commerce.[1] The *Cédula de Gracias al Sacar* of 1815 was an open invitation to people from both Europe and the Americas to settle in Puerto Rico.

Immigrants had been drawn to the island even before the 1815 document was published. The turbulent years at the turn of the nineteenth century set whites, free people of color, and slaves adrift in the Atlantic World. During the Spanish domination of Puerto Rico, a foreigner was simply defined as a person who originated from a country or territory other than Puerto Rico. *Peninsulares* (those who originated from the Iberian Peninsula), Spanish subjects from other territories in the Americas, and émigrés from non-Spanish dominions were all groups included in the expansion of Puerto Rico. To relocate into the Puerto Rican territory required the proper authorization. Reasons for immigrating were numerous and cut across national, economic, racial, and gender lines. The motivation of men and women to relocate stemmed from their need or desire to have a better quality of life, which required them to leave family, friends, and often all material possesions behind. There were both voluntary and forced moves throughout the Caribbean and immigrants' reasons varied based on the situation. The need to better one's condition in life, change a stagnant life, escape a life of poverty, increase employment opportunities, or achieve social advancement were all specific factors for migrating. Social reasons were of equal importance to political and ideological reasons, such as change of government, revolution, and persecution for political or religious ideas.

Puerto Rican historical scholarship has often given the false impression that the majority of the foreigners settling on the island due to the *Cédula* were landowners who were both wealthy and white. A thorough investigation reveals that in addition to the well-known dominant culture, there was also an important group of workers and artisans who occupied the middle and lower levels of the economic ladder. Among immigrant landowners, workers, and artisans were free people of color who contributed fully to the economy and culture of their adopted land, which is a fact often forgotten.

Although scholarship on slavery in the Atlantic World has significantly expanded in the recent years, the study of free people of color within the world of slavery is still an oft-overlooked subject. Within the context of Spanish America, scholars have tended to focus on the larger colonies of Mexico, Peru, or Cuba.[2] Very little attention has been granted to Puerto Rico or its inhabitants during the era of slavery (which lasted until 1873). Only recently has a small, but critical, body of work emerged that explores Puerto Ricans of African descent, both enslaved or free.[3] During the nineteenth century, the population of free people of color grew considerably on the island. Since the majority of authors concentrated on the slave society and the slave population, they failed to consider the major role of free people of color in the society.[4]

Puerto Rico was uniquely different from any other Caribbean plantation society; therefore, the omission is important in reflecting the true culture of the island. The demographics in Puerto Rico were considerably different than assumed by most scholars in the research of slavery and race relations in the Atlantic World. In the early nineteenth century, like most populations in the region, the island had a colored majority. In Puerto Rico, the percentage of free people of color was a consistently large part of the *total* population.

Within the larger Caribbean slave society, the proportions of free people of color varied from colony to colony. In San Domingue (Haiti), just before the 1789 revolution, free people of color were 45 percent of the free population. In that same year, free people of color in Martinique constituted one-third of the total free population; however, both of those societies found the free colored population greatly outnumbered by the slave population. The free colored population hovered around a scant five percent of the *total* island population in the French colonies of Martinique and San Domingue. In Jamaica and Barbados, the two most important of the British Caribbean colonies, free people of color made up an even smaller percentage of the total population in the late eighteenth century: two percent and one percent respectively[5] (see table 3–1).[6]

The Spanish Caribbean provided a contrast to the British and French colonies. Cuba and Puerto Rico had a long history of white settlement that, unlike many other European colonies, predated the advent of the plantation economy. In 1774, Cuba's free people of color represented 27 percent of the total free population and 21 percent of the total island population.[7] Even within the Caribbean, Puerto Rico's demographics stood out. In 1775, free people of color comprised 49 percent of the total island population, thus making them the largest group on the island. Of the total free population, they constituted an incredible 54 percent[8] (see table 3–2).[9]

Throughout the nineteenth century, the majority of people of African descent living in Puerto Rico were free, and only a minority of them had ever been enslaved. At the turn of the century, free people of color constituted a near majority segment of the *total* Puerto Rican population: 42 percent in 1797, 40 percent in 1820, and 46 percent in 1834. By the middle of the nineteenth century, the free colored population consistently constituted over 40 percent of Puerto Rico's total population. In 1850, the total free population of the island consisted of almost 85 percent of the total population, thus, making the free population numerically the most important group. The statistics indicate that of the total free population in 1850, free people of color constituted 45 percent.[10] By contrast, during the first half of the nineteenth century, the Puerto Rican slave population averaged only 12 percent of the total population and never climbed above 16 percent[11] (See table 3–3).[12]

In the Caribbean, limitations placed on free colored populations varied in degree of severity and enforcement. In the French colonies, there were increasing restrictions on the civil rights of free people of color during the course of the eighteenth century. The restrictions contradicted the seventeenth century legal code, the *Code Noir*, which granted full citizenship rights to all manumitted slaves and allowed legal and social liberties for free people of color. White colonists in the French Caribbean, however, systematically disregarded the *Code Noir*; as a result, eighteenth-century regulations toward free people of color grew increasingly explicit in their restrictiveness. Gwendolyn Midlo Hall suggested that the Haitian Revolution was precipitated by a free colored population reacting to whites who degraded them socially, attempted to strip them of legal protection, and destroy their network of influence.[13] In San Domingue, restrictive legislation included depriving free colored landowners of their property, limiting participation of free people of color in colonial politics, and outlawing marriages between white and free people of color.

Similar restrictive laws were found in other parts of the Caribbean, and this legislation against free people of color was often invasive and regularly stymied or curtailed movement in daily activities. On the French and the Danish islands, there were laws restricting the clothes free people of color could wear. Certain items were prohibited, including silk stockings and other clothing made of silk, chintz, jewelry, and gold and silver brocade.[14] In Martinique, free women of color were forbidden from wearing silk petticoats. A "petticoat patrol," usually consisting of white males, stood guard at church doors and social functions to lift skirts to check for compliance. To spare everyone the embarrassment, free women of color started the practice of tucking a corner of their overskirts into their waistbands to assist the patrolmen.[15]

The white inhabitants on the British islands expressed concern about the free colored class gaining wealth. The Jamaican Assembly passed restrictive laws to reduce the possibility of free people of color becoming as rich as members of the white plantocracy. The laws imposed a limit on the dollar amount for bequests given to free people of color by white benefactors. The Grenada Assembly blocked attempts by free people of color to buy land or house lots in towns. White citizens on the British Virgin Islands imposed a special tax to restrict slaveholding by free people of color. In Saint Kitts, free colored children could not attend public schools even if their parents were taxpayers.[16]

Free people of color were subjected to curfews in an effort to monitor their movements and stem potential subversive actions. They experienced segregation in churches where special seating arrangements separated white and black parishioners. Free people of color were required to attend separate performances at the theater or were seated separately at the show. Most disconcerting of all, free people of color faced a constant threat of being re-enslaved and always had to prove they were free.[17] In sum, throughout most of the Caribbean, free people of color were allowed a civil status little removed from that of slaves. Restrictions were designed to limit civil rights, restrict economic possibilities, and curtail the social interactions of free people of color.

Though each island had its own nuances, Arnold Sio describes a consciousness among free people of color found throughout the Caribbean. Free people of color regularly developed as a distinct group. According to Sio, their sense of identity presented itself in three ways: in definitions of acceptable behavior among themselves; in the terms by which they defined themselves; and in their views of themselves in relation to whites, slaves, a particular island; and to the Caribbean region as a whole. Sio concluded that limitations on the economic development of Caribbean free people of color kept them marginal to the main economy of their given society, which led to the rise of a group consciousness, independent from that of their white counterparts.[18] By contrast, both the white and the black free populations of Puerto Rico found themselves outside the economic structure of the society. Group consciousness became one of nation building rather than color divisions. Ideas of abolition, local self-rule, and full independence grew in both populations side by side, without regard to the color of the skin.

Puerto Rico's free people of color were provided an impressive degree of legal protection, notwithstanding the restrictive 1848 edict of Governor Prim.[19] In terms of their participation in Puerto Rico's market economy, two legal rights were especially significant. Puerto Rico's free people of color had access to the courts and the town councils. For a great majority of the island's general population, the most crucial courts were the small claims courts, which made access to the aforementioned municipal agencies pertinent. All civil cases for sums less than 400 pesos were heard by the local *alcaldes* and resolved verbally.[20] In the absence of resolution, cases were taken to a higher level for appeal. Small claims courts were utilized by artisans, storekeepers, and others with legal problems involving money. Town councils were vital; they were charged with supervising small retail stores, artisan shops, general business practices (what might and might not be sold, hours, prices), setting weights and measures, and other compliances. Additionally, town councils were the immediate supervisory agencies for the artisan guilds, controlling matters such as the nature of membership, election of officers, and testing and certification of master craftsmen. A free person of color could appear in front of the town officials to request the purchase or rental of a piece of land owned by the town. A group of free people of color could come forward to redress a labor grievance. The color of one's skin was not a stipulation for addressing the town council or from receiving recourse from the board.

For the twenty-first-century historian, utilizing these tribunal sources can be problematic. While the tribunal records are a rich source for exploring social interactions in the emerging market economy, they do not refer to the race of the participants. This omission demonstrates that in the Puerto Rican context, the color of the participant was not as important as the case that was brought before the local tribunal. On the contrary, the lack of delineation by color makes it difficult to use these records for the purpose of this study.

Perhaps this is because Puerto Rico was *not* a center of dynamic economic activity and opportunity; by law, free people of color could live where they wanted and enter most occupations, including all the artisanal trades. The reality, however, was that very few people of color could be found at the higher ranks of business. While a nineteenth-century version of "the glass ceiling" existed for free people of color, race was not always the determinant factor in social advancement. Tenacity, pure doggedness, and acceptance by white compatriots enabled many free people of color, in Puerto Rico, to overcome what might have been insurmountable odds in other Caribbean plantation societies.[21]

There were limitations placed on Puerto Rico's free people of color, yet most of the social constraints found on other islands did not seem to apply to this community. Sio's suggestion that limitations on economic development kept free people of color marginal is not a valid assertion for Puerto Rico. Puerto Rico was not a racial utopia; but in spite of tensions that persisted in Puerto Rico and elsewhere in the Caribbean during the late eighteenth and early nineteenth centuries, the coexistence of rural free people of color and poor whites in this fledgling plantation society helped alleviate societal stresses on the island.

The early years of the nineteenth century saw a diverse group of free people of color migrating to Puerto Rico. Like white immigrants, they were taking advantage of favorable immigration policies and an auspicious social climate. The native population of free people of color tended to be rural and survive through subsistence agriculture. By contrast, the majority of immigrants of color settled in the towns and cities along the coast, and few ventured inland to the mountainous areas of the island. Due to blacks and whites intermingling in the general population, most immigrants soon became culturally indistinguishable from their native counterparts. A vast number of the new immigrants of color had marketable trades, having previously worked as carpenters, shoemakers, sailors, artisans, seamstresses, tailors, merchants, small shopkeepers, laundresses, or street vendors. Many were literate; some spoke more than one language.[21] They came from places such as Guadeloupe, San Domingue, Caracas, Saint Thomas, Costa Firme (Venezuela), and Colombia. Escaping revolutions in the South Americas, racial strife on the French islands, economic hardship, or lack of social mobility, they were searching for a better quality of life for themselves and their families.

Records from six towns around the island (Aguada, Aguadilla, Añasco, Cabo Rojo, Patillas, and Rincón) offer enticing glimpses into the lives of both native and immigrant free people of color, which included the development of a snapshot of daily life in early nineteenth-century Puerto Rico. Each town yields a different piece of the fabric; when the quilt is put together, it gives a unique view of the social construction of the island in the opening years of the nineteenth century.

Immigrant and Native Free People of Color

Aguadilla was a town with a large concentration of both native free people of color and immigrant free people of color. It was a relatively new town in the early nineteenth century, having only been founded in the late 1770s. Plantains, coffee, tobacco, and sugar cane were the main agriculture products used both for subsistence and trade. Almost all the inhabitants were involved in either the agricultural or fishing industries. It makes sense that Aguadilla would be a mecca for immigrants; the town was prominently situated on a coastal plain. The natural harbor had long been utilized by ships as a water collection stop and was now quickly becoming a lucrative trading port.

The 1820s saw a large influx of immigrants of all colors mainly from Costa Firme and Hispañola to this flourishing town on Puerto Rico's northwestern coast. An 1825 census showed 235 of the town's 1,333 inhabitants (17 percent) had arrived within the last fifteen years. The bourgeoning town included a total of 74 houses and 216 huts spread out over miles of hills and plains.[22]

Immigrant free people of color in Aguadilla offered a variety of practical skills. Within the ranks of the recently arrived in the early nineteenth century were four cobblers, three tailors, a sailor, and four small farmers. Vincente Morel arrived from Santo Domingo in 1818; he carried his skills as a cobbler along with his wife and three children. His neighbor, Juan Enrique Eliger, also a shoemaker, arrived from Curaçao that same year with his wife and five children. Adding to the ranks of skilled free colored immigrants were three tailors from Curaçao who arrived between 1829 and 1830.[23] By the time of the 1830 census, none of the tailors had been in Puerto Rico more than six months.

While the shoemakers and tailors arrived in Puerto Rico as free men, two of the four immigrant farmers in Aguadilla actually arrived in Puerto Rico as slaves in 1816. They were freed within a year of arrival, although there is no record as to why or how they were granted their freedom. By 1826, both former slaves owned small plots of land on which they lived with their growing families.[24] Hard work and consistent output helped them become accepted members of the community and alleviated the stigma of their former civil status.

Guadeloupian sailor Mateo Montesino lived in Aguadilla for twenty-six years by 1830. He arrived in 1804 before the open invitation of the 1815 *Cédula de Gracias al Sacar* and after major hostilities on his home island had cooled. He settled into a home, raised a family, and continued to go to sea on the many ships that passed through the busy port.[25] Travel within the Caribbean could be a tedious event; ships coming from southern ports, such as Curaçao, often had to tack against strong trade winds to reach northern destinations such as Puerto Rico. This could add days to a journey on ships with cramped quarters, filled with tired and disoriented immigrants. The difficult travel conditions must have been a strain on the health of cobbler Nicolas Was. Nicolas, his wife Isabel, and his brother Francisco arrived just three months before the 1830 census. An unusual debarkation document indicates Nicolas was suffering from an undisclosed illness at the time of his arrival. Rather than the usual recourse of quarantining him or putting him on the next ship back to Curaçao, the customs official remanded him to the care of his wife Isabel for the duration of his illness.[26] If he did not recover, he was to be sent back to Curaçao. Presumably Nicolas recovered since he was found as head-of-household in subsequent Aguadilla census reports.

As the above examples demonstrate, immigrants of color were able to come to Puerto Rico and firmly situate themselves into their new environments due to having marketable skills. Other examples of long-established free colored immigrants around the island include two forty-five-year-old laborers from San Domingue and thirty-eight-year-old sailor Jacob Porriel. These men all married Puerto Rican women from the free colored community, and, after living thirty years in Puerto Rico, they were well-entrenched in the community. Marrying Puerto Ricans secured their place within island society and cemented relationships within the community.

The Efre brothers, shoemakers from Curaçao, owned and shared the maintenance and employee costs of a carpentry shop in the bustling town center of Aguadilla. The older brother had been in Puerto Rico for twelve years and the younger for seven. There were two more shops in the neighborhood owned by Fernando Ambias and Antonio Paterson. They were twenty-five-year-old carpenters from Martinique and Saint Thomas, respectively. All four of these artisans established a secure trade pattern within the community, thus building their status and lending a sense of belonging and perpetuity.

In the northwestern coastal town of Arecibo, an active little community of approximately nine square miles, one could find over 200 houses and cottages in the main town and another 1,200 residences in the outlying areas. The major industries in 1838 were livestock and agriculture with the predominant crops being sugar cane, coffee, plantains, tobacco, corn, rice, and various beans.[27] Arecibo's most prominent feature was a lighthouse perched on a rocky promontory from which lookouts could spot passing ships. The lighthouse, El Morrillo, helped Arecibo serve as a major lookout point for pirates and sea attacks on the northwestern side of the island.

As in Aguadilla, this bustling seaside town of Arecibo must have been a big attraction for newly immigrated families. Ships anchoring in the bay needed tailors to repair tattered uniforms, carpenters for major repairs, *tornaleros* (lathe operators) for furniture repair and intricate woodworking, merchants with whom they could trade their goods and purchase supplies, and shoemakers to replace leather straps and footwear destroyed by saltwater. The sea trade was also a good way to get timely news of events happening throughout the Caribbean and the world.

This vibrant and growing town had a population of 10,000 in 1824. The majority of the town population was engaged in agriculture and raising livestock outside the town limits. The town center boasted twelve carpenters, ten shoemakers, three blacksmiths, three bricklayers, and thirty-three medium and small-scale merchants.

Immigrants of color held prominent jobs in this seaside town. Bernando Dupont came to Puerto Rico as a child and became a naturalized citizen in 1816. By 1826, he was married, had his own child, and owned a carpentry shop.[28] Of Arecibo's twelve carpenters, three, including Dupont, were free people of color. *Tornaleros*, artisans who fashioned or shaped objects on a lathe, comprised another important trade in this seaside economy. Two of the five *tornaleros* in Arecibo, Juan Haris Yambo and Luis Nicolas Roldan, were free men of color. As a caulker, *pardo* Pedro Ramirez's job was to repair the cracks in a ship's hull to keep it watertight; a pretty important skill in a portside town. He had arrived from Santa Marta in 1798 and was well established in his trade by 1826.[29]

Arecibo also boasted two free colored tailors and a free colored shoemaker. Curaçao native Guillermo Gogue was one of the town's ten shoemakers. His neighbors, Luis Lorant and Juan Bautista Busman, were tailors who had both emigrated from the British island of Dominica in 1810. Lorant became prosperous enough to own a tailor shop and three slaves to help him with production and distribution. It was not unusual for Arecibo's free people of color to own slaves, as recorded in the nominal slave census of 1826. Of the 110 slave owners listed, forty (36 percent) were free people of color. They owned 38 percent of the recorded slaves with an average of 2.7 slaves per owner. These numbers demonstrate an integration of free people of color into the economic and social fabric of the Puerto Rican and the greater Caribbean society.

Moving farther down the western coast of Puerto Rico, we find the town of Añasco. A close look at one of its six neighborhoods, Río Arríba, illuminates a community comprised of twenty families of whites, *pardos,* and blacks. The community itself was well integrated with white families and families of color living as housemates, neighbors, and spouses. In this microcosm of Puerto Rican society, over 40 percent of the families were mixed marriages, and there was no apparent residential segregation based on income or color.[30]

It is enlightening to look inside the households of Río Arríba and see how they were racially and socially structured. Census data this detailed are rare in Puerto Rico, and this neighborhood offers an unusual view inside the homes of average Puerto Ricans. Glimpses such as this contradict the assertions of historian Jay Kinsbruner, who claimed racial prejudice placed insidious limitations on the social development of Puerto Rico and that racial stratification was imposed from all levels of society throughout the island.[31] The neighborhood of Río Arríba refutes these claims.

The census in colonial Latin America was very dependent on the census taker. He was the eyes and ears of the Crown. Colonies were mandated to submit a census or *padrón* of their inhabitants on a regular cycle. They were taken for population studies, taxation purposes, military purposes, and agricultural assessments, and were evaluated at various levels of the government. The racial categories in the census were highly subjective. Recording the color of a citizen was dependent on how the census taker perceived each citizen. The census taker might impose his views onto the individual when classifying the person. The information was not always provided by the person, which caused some inconsistencies. The information might be given to a census taker by any member of the family or even by a neighbor. As census takers walked their rounds, they unwittingly preserved the complex tapestry of everyday life and often in ways that cannot be duplicated by other sources. While truly a mix of random bits of information, the census records give a snapshot of a society from that particular time.

An interesting feature of the Río Arríba census was the separate category for enumerating *agregados*. *Agregados* were in some cases simply
boarders who came from the countryside and paid room and board.
Quite often, these *agregados* were relatives who came to live with family
in town. Single sisters with children would sometimes live with siblings in another town. Younger brothers and sisters were often sent to
live and work with siblings or cousins in towns where the economy
was better. *Pardo* couple Atilano Ponce and his wife, Tomasa de Jesus,
had two *agregados*, Juana de Jesus and Eugenia Sanchez, living with
them. Judging by the ages of Juana and Eugenia, the *agregados* were
probably Tomasa's sister and niece. The curious twist here is that Juana
and her daughter are listed as white by the census taker.[32] If Tomasa
and Juana were sisters, it was the census taker who viewed them separately. This is a good example of the subjectivity of race classification.

Don Ignacio Ruiz, a thirty-nine-year-old widower, lived in Río
Arríba with four boys, three girls, and a large number of free servants.
His neighbor, Don Dionicio Torres, had seven total non–family members listed in his household. Both Ruiz and Torres were white and had
children and *agregados* living with them. In addition to his two teen-
aged *agregados*, one white and one *pardo*, Ruiz also had eighteen free
servants, all of whom were *pardos*. Rita, his oldest servant, was 110
years old. In Torres' case, all five *agregados* were white, and his free
servants were a sixty-year-old white woman and a thirty-two-year-old
parda named, oddly enough, Dionicia Torres.

Don Manuel Nieves was white, married, and had eight children.
Also in his household were five slaves and two young *agregados*, one
white and one *pardo*. It is an interesting commentary that in this neighborhood of twenty families of varied racial and economic status, Don
Nieves is the only one who owned slaves.

A Glimpse at the Women

Parsing out the lives of free people of color in Puerto Rico can be difficult, and trying to uncover the lives of the women is even more of
a challenge. In general, records from the early nineteenth century

in Puerto Rico are spotty or incomplete. They often offer tantalizing previews, but rarely a complete picture of the lives these women of color led. An unusual glimpse of female immigrants of color can be found in an 1830 register for Aguadilla and the neighboring town of Aguada. With only two exceptions, the women had been in Puerto Rico less than five years, with the shortest stay being one month. It appears that in these municipalities the majority of the women were going through the relocation process alone. Thirty-three-year-old Vuelemina Ferrer was a very recent immigrant, having only arrived from Curaçao with her three young children one month before the 1830 register was taken.

Another free colored female immigrant from Curaçao was Catalina Ricardo. Along with her daughter Constanza Henrrique, she owned a small grocery store (*ventorrillo*) for which she obtained a license in 1830. Catalina's *ventorrillo* was a small establishment, which probably sold locally produced fruits, vegetables, and low-quality spirits. In his book, *Women and Urban Change in San Juan, Puerto Rico*, Félix Matos Rodríguez found that the majority of *ventorrillo* owners were women and that free women of color most often operated this particular type of store. Matos Rodríguez's book focused on the compact urban capital city, so it is interesting to see his findings carry through to the more sparsely populated interior towns. *Ventorrillos* required a very small capital outlay, so they were easier to establish.[33] Using local produce meant low overhead costs, while staying in business required making and maintaining contacts with local producers as well as building a loyal clientele in the community. As a free woman of color, Catalina's business success depended on her acceptance within the community as a whole.

A much larger establishment was owned by Maria Alejandrina Alers. She had been in Puerto Rico since 1808, and she and her family were firmly established in the fabric of the community. The Alers family owned at least two houses, one in the city center of Aguada and another, apparently, on the property of a large hacienda in Aguadilla. They also owned one of the three large mercantile stores (*comercio*) in Aguada, of which Maria was the proprietor. In 1838, six slaves were registered to the Alers family in Aguada, and Maria was listed as owning of four of them. Three of her four slaves helped Maria run the store in Aguada while her brother managed the *hacienda* outside of Aguadilla.[34]

Comercios were an important economic link in the community, and the biggest type of store found in the colony. A *comerciante* was the owner and operator of the *comercio*. There were very few women to be found at this level of the mercantile business. Most women, and most women of color, owned smaller stores like Catalina's *ventorrillo* due to the small capital outlay necessary to establish and run the business. The *comercio* had the largest, and usually the best, supply of household goods and personal items desired by the townspeople. *Comercios* were also the primary suppliers of clothing, agricultural implements, and food necessary for the maintenance of the *haciendas* and smaller farms in the area. Maria Alejandrina's proprietorship of the general store suggests a keen ability to work with people of all races and genders on the island. The fact that a woman of color was able to establish herself in an elite mercantile group demonstrates a certain amount of pliability in the social system.

In 1838, Rincón was a sleepy coastal town that fit snugly in the foothills of La Cadena Mountains. Its reef-lined Atlantic beaches boasted migrating whales that attracted whalers in the eighteenth and nineteenth centuries, and they are now known as some of the Caribbean's best surfing beaches. Ships would anchor off the calmer Caribbean beaches and row supplies in to the town.

The Rincón census gives us insight into the lives of free people of color through their jobs and marital status and provides a glimpse of free women of color. The *Padrón de Pardos* ("Census of Free People of Color") for the town is intact and fairly extensive.[35] A comparison of the white and *pardo* residents of Rincón in 1838 is not possible because there is no extant census of the white population or available record of any mixed marriages. Apparently, all of the free people of color were considered *pardo* for the purpose of this census, so there is no color delineation even within the free colored population. We know that there were 431 *pardos* listed in this census and that there were 80 *pardo* households represented in Rincón's seven neighborhoods.

The census recorded all the members of the household of working age. The initial year of work appeared to be between the ages of eleven and sixteen. Of the 231 entries under occupation, ninety-four percent were listed as *labradors* (small farmer). The occupations of the other five percent included four landlords, two carpenters, a shoemaker, a seamstress, and a midwife.

The 1838 Rincón census included three women and one man in the role of *casero* (landlord or administrator). It is not clear exactly what type of property these women kept, or even if they owned the property, but since two of these women were married to carpenters, it is quite possible they owned the property in which their husbands' shops were located. Twenty-five-year old Guadalupe Sanchez had three children, ages one, four, and six. She was also one of the few *parda* Rincón women who had an *agregado* living in her home. Twelve-year-old Jose Sanchez was probably a nephew or brother who helped Guadalupe and her husband, Francisco Allende, around the house. It could also be assumed that he was an apprentice in Francisco's carpentry shop.

Octavia Arroyo did not have an *agregado* living on her property, but she did have the benefit of her twenty-year-old son, Juan, still at home. This *labrador* worked alongside his father, Francisco LaCruz, in the carpentry shop as an apprentice. The other children, ages nine, eleven, and twelve, would begin contributing to the family business soon, if they had not already. This was not unusual, because children began work at a young age in the early nineteenth-century Atlantic World. Child labor laws were practically nonexistent.[28] Children were needed to help bring money and food to the household. Large families were the norm, not only for financial reasons, but because the child mortality rate was so high. One of the most famous paintings by celebrated Puerto Rican artist, Francisco Manuel Oller y Cestero, *El Velorio* (1893), depicts the wake of a young child. Due to infant mortality, accidents, and childhood diseases, the percentage of children living to adulthood in nineteenth-century Puerto Rico was less than 50.

The town midwife, the only one of any color in the 1838 Rincon census, was Ana la Rosa, a fifty-year-old single mother from the Dominican Republic. As midwife, she performed one of the most important jobs in the social fabric of the community. She saw the birth of hundreds of children, and it is highly likely that both the white and free colored community utilized her much-needed services. Physicians were rare outside major urban centers, and their care was also an expensive luxury most Puerto Ricans could not afford. Lack of hospitals and trained physicians made midwives indispensable for most births. Midwives helped provide an effective and efficient health service to pregnant women and were an integral part of the medical system for centuries. They were also the traditional healers of the community, serving in the absence of licensed physicians. It is interesting that Ana la Rosa was an outsider, an immigrant from the Dominican Republic. Healers were usually long-established community members who inherited their posts from older established women, but la Rosa had been in Río Arríba since 1812; therefore, her presence must have been validated by the community.

The Spanish government tried to regulate midwives and other non-professional practitioners of medicine. In 1838, the salaries of midwives, doctors, surgeons, and bloodletters were set by the government. Due to the scarcity of obstetricians, colonial officials ordered that midwives should be allowed to perform natural births on their own. By 1838, Ana la Rosa had probably helped to see two generations of Rincón residents born, including her own grandchildren.

Rosalia Gonzalez cooked out of her home or worked outside the home as a cook in a restaurant or a private home. The label *cocinera* means she was the proprietor of her own restaurant or café. Seventy-five-year-old Venezuelan shoemaker Jose Francisco Velásquez was married to Puerto Rican Guadalupe Allende. Velásquez's wife Guadalupe, like Rosalia's husband Pedro Gonzalez, was listed as a *labrador*. As Rosalia and Jose Francisco worked in their given trades, Guadalupe and Pedro must have been responsible for tending the crops to sustain Rosalia's cooking trade and their families.

Catalina Cornel was a sixty-one-year-old single woman who, by 1838, had been in Puerto Rico for forty years. Originally from Saint Thomas, Catalina had arrived in Puerto Rico as the slave of Patricio Hernandez. She was freed soon after her arrival and settled in Cabo

Rojo working a small plot of land. The other freed slave on the immigrant roster was Juan Baptista Leon, a shoemaker. He was brought to the island from Saint Bartholomew and freed in 1819.

The lives of women did not always fit into a neat compartment. Some women stood out because of positive attributes, contributions, or their collaborative efforts as stated above; however, in the case of Agustina Ortiz, deviant behavior was exhibited. In March of 1817, a plea requesting immediate action against one of its citizens was presented to the military commander of the hillside town of Toa Alta. The widow Agustina Ortiz, a free *parda*, seemed to be causing a ruckus in her little town by stealing turkeys, appropriating fancy clothes, and causing general disturbances at odd hours of the night. The townspeople were fed up with her antics and further worried that her daughter, Maria Ramirez, might be party to her mother's thievery.[36]

Agustina had at three strikes against her: she was a free *parda*, a widow, and allegedly a military widow. Her defense to her accusers was that her widow's pension was not being delivered, so she was left with no viable means of support. Agustina was not alone in her financial plight. Spain was notoriously bad about paying decent wages to its military—or even paying them on time. Widows and children were at the bottom of the disbursement list and often would go months and sometimes years without payment.[37] For some women, pensions added financial resources to a well-established inheritance or family wealth. For others, like Agustina Ortiz, pensions were the difference between barely making ends meet and not surviving at all.[38] It was not uncommon for widows to petition their local military garrison for financial relief. There were plenty of pleading letters describing starving children and desolate mothers waiting patiently, albeit in vain, for their tardy checks.[39]

Both white and free colored women were affected, but free women of color, like Agustina, were less likely to find a satisfactory resolution to their problem.[40] Agustina decided she would not be a victim and chose to take matters into her own hands, much to the chagrin of her neighbors. When Rosa Figueroa's best holiday dress and silk shoes went missing, only to be found in that "den of wickedness," she

finally had enough of her wayward neighbor.[41] Agustina was ordered
to leave Toa Alta within three days. Her response was to thumb her
nose at the judge then reply that she would not be run out of town.
Military officials and townspeople were exasperated with Agustina's
stubbornness. The military official to whom the case was first presented sent a pleading letter to officials in San Juan asking for a quick and
satisfactory solution.[42] Unfortunately, there is no record of a response
from garrison headquarters.

A loss of revenue, such as a military pension, could send a family into desperation. Women and free people of color were especially
vulnerable to the vagaries of the Spanish pension system. During the
eighteenth and nineteenth centuries, the military was an ever-present
institution in the Caribbean. For free people of color, it could be either
a way for advancement or a study in discrimination. The military in
Puerto Rico was reorganized in 1765 into nineteen infantry and five
cavalry units. At the turn of the nineteenth century, four of those infantry companies were reserved for free men of color. Within these companies, they could become both commissioned and noncommissioned
officers.[43]

Both white and free colored militia were outfitted with the same
armaments, which included musket, bayonet, and short saber. By arm-
ing the free colored troops the same as the white troops, the Spanish
government was demonstrating the important role free soldiers of col-
or were expected to play in the defense of the island. Also, free colored
militia were entitled to military jurisdiction in both civil and criminal
matters, thereby not being subject to the local jurisdiction of the town
councils.

Military life was not easy; desertions and absences from required
drills were commonplace among both white and free colored militias.
It eventually became difficult for the free colored militia units to fill
their ranks. In 1842, each of the four free colored infantry troops was
required to have 100 men on their volunteer military roster. But on
October 1 of that year, the San Juan company reported seventy-two
men on its roster. Cangrejos had forty-eight, Vega Baja had thirty-six,
and Bayamón had a dismal thirty-one volunteers.

Labor and Land

Even in the nineteenth century, the majority of Puerto Ricans lived in villages and small towns with an average population of fewer than 4,000 inhabitants. Over 70 percent of the population in Puerto Rico was illiterate, and few had marketable trades. In addition to subsistence farming, Puerto Rican peasants worked occasionally on the farms and plantations of large landowners. The 1838 census of Rincón offers a glimpse into the occupations of average Puerto Ricans. The census indicates that free people of color were involved in a variety of trades that served the needs of the community at large. It highlights the dependence on subsistence farming in Puerto Rico's economy. Ninety-five percent of the Rincon's free people of color were subsistence farmers.

The study of free labor versus slave labor is a growing area in nineteenth-century Puerto Rican historiography. Among the most cited of early sources on Puerto Rican labor is the 1834 report of George Flinter. This study, and the studies that were later based on it, maintained that free laborers and slaves worked in harmony under the paternal guidance of the plantation owners. Flinter and subsequent studies contended that free workers performed most of the work on the *haciendas*, due to the small number of slaves. The study concluded that the slave population in Puerto Rico rarely exceeded 12 percent and that slave labor had only a marginal impact on the island economy.[44] Flinter's personal observations led him to claim that in the daily struggle for survival, the slaves were better off than the free workers. His rationale was that the slaves had their basic needs covered by the master, while the free laborers only had themselves to depend on for sustenance. In Flinter's conclusion, Puerto Rican slavery was a benevolent institution that was a desirable alternative to the chaos and poverty experienced by the free laborers on the island.

While Joel Poinsett's visit was a sightseeing side trip, the objective of Flinter's 1834 visit to Puerto Rico was to explore the consequences to the continuance of Spanish slavery. It was at a time when the British government was trying to enforce its treaty with Spain regarding the cessation of the slave trade in the Caribbean. Flinter's accounts were designed as propaganda, at a time when slavery in the Americas was coming under severe abolitionist pressure in his native Britain. Flinter defended Spanish slavery on the islands of Cuba and Puerto Rico by stating that slavery in Puerto Rico was of minimal importance to the island's export economy. He advocated that it was easy on the slaves due to "wise and philanthropic" provisions of the Spanish slave codes. Flinter explained the "insignificance of slave imports" in the 1820s and 1830s not by publicizing the clandestine slave trade that was the real reason for the dramatic increase in the slave population on the island but by portraying the material and family conditions of the slaves in the best light possible.[45] He asserted that the harsh conditions that normally limited the slave population from reproducing itself did not exist on the island. What Flinter failed to tell his readers was that between 1813 and 1828 the annual rate of increase of Puerto Rico's slave population was just over four percent. Such a rate of increase would have been difficult to explain simply on the basis of normal reproduction.

Not surprisingly, recent studies of sugar plantations and the lives of slaves have called into question the assertions of orderly and contented slave populations made by Flinter. Benjamin Nistal-Moret, in his book *Esclavos Prófugos y Cimarrones*, makes available a wealth of data about hundreds of runaway slaves who willingly exchanged their lives as slaves for the unknown risks of the mountains. Guillermo Baralt's study, *Esclavos Rebeldes*, found that during the eighteenth and nineteenth centuries, Puerto Rican slaves organized revolts, set fire to cane fields, and killed their masters and overseers. Both studies show that in planning quests for freedom, slaves in Puerto Rico risked being apprehended, severely punished in jail, or killed for their efforts, just as they did throughout the Atlantic World.[46]

Authors Francisco Scarano and Andres Ramos Mattei question Flinter's assertion that Puerto Rico's sugar industry relied more on free labor than on slave labor. Their studies of the sugar *haciendas* in southwestern Puerto Rico conclude that slaves were the primary source of labor on large estates and that free laborers provided only supplementary labor.[47] The study also indicates that free laborers tended to be hired by the smaller estates, which lacked the large number of slaves to plant, cut, and process the cane. The smaller estates, however, were in the majority in Puerto Rico.

Planters regularly complained that even when free workers were willing to work on the estates, they did not work the fully allotted time. They were prone to take off as soon as they had earned enough to supplement the output from their subsistence plots. Puerto Rico had a large population of peasants who remained on the periphery of the plantation economy. In 1844, the British consul to Puerto Rico commented that the "natives who are free surpass by far the slaves; many possess small plots in which they live." He added that "they only cultivate that which they find necessary to sustain themselves; they care little about improving their crops or their condition."[48]

There had been a growing number of settlers scattered around the arid plains of the Patillas valley since the middle of the eighteenth century. The town of Patillas was founded in 1811. The immediate reason for founding the town was the establishment small sugar mills in the valley, which stimulated the cultivation of sugar cane. Doña Adelana Citrón established a *hacienda* and donated almost eight acres of land to the new town. In 1828, Patillas had 4,135 inhabitants, of whom 48 percent were free people of color. Another 28 percent were white and 10 percent were slaves. The other 14 percent were *agregados* for whom no racial classification was given. By 1845, the free colored population jumped to 61 percent and the slave population rose to 13 percent, while the white population fell to 26 percent.[49]

Our best glimpse of this new community, one in which two-thirds of the free population was classified as free *mulato* or free *negro*, comes from the 1812 census. Eighty-five percent of the free colored families in Patillas owned more than two acres of pasture land, with an average of 8.3 acres per family. They also owned an average of 1.1 cows and 2.3 horses per family. This community was very dependent on the fruits of the land.[50]

In terms of crops, only four families in Patillas planted cotton and three families planted sugar. These are the high-profit crops, which points to an economy fueled by small producers. Even the sugar farmers had low yields, since sugar growers planted less than an acre each.

In a town founded in relation to sugar mills, it is very interesting that only six free colored families produced raw molasses for sugar production. In turn, it should also be noted that only 2 percent of the white population produced any sugar products and less than half worked more than one acre of cane.

One reason for this low sugar yield in what was to become a major sugar-producing region is that the cultivation of sugar cane in Puerto Rico did not begin to expand until the second and third decades of the nineteenth century. Until that time, most growers were small-scale producers. The majority of Puerto Ricans, regardless of color, could not raise enough capital to invest in the machinery, nor the slaves required to begin commercial sugar production. There were few Puerto Ricans who had practical experience with the sophisticated methods and techniques necessary for large-scale cultivation and processing. Barely a handful of sugar *haciendas* were in existence on the entire island before 1815, so there were few opportunities to train in managerial and technical occupations related to the processing of cane. San Domingue was the source of many of the skilled sugar processors. The refugees of the revolt were slow to immigrate to Puerto Rico, electing instead to settle in Cuba, Louisiana, or even the other French islands before choosing Puerto Rico. The 1815 Cédula was the key to opening the door to these talented émigrés.

The majority of free colored families in Patillas produced plantains, coffee, corn, and rice on their land. On average, each family cultivated 1.67 acres of plantains and 1,551 feet of coffee per year. Annually, the average yield per household was 6.7 pounds of coffee, 1.9 bags of rice, and 770 pounds of corn. It appears that coffee and rice were mainly subsistence crops, but that corn was a main crop raised for sale.[51]

Puerto Rico was still very much a peasant society at the start of the nineteenth century, and the island's economy was dominated by peasant forms of production. Scarano suggests that the increases in per capita food production and a steep rise in the rate of natural increase of the rural population after 1765 reinforced the economic foundations of the peasant society.[35] By 1830, there were 10,770 acres of land in sugar cane in Puerto Rico, 8,730 acres in coffee, and just over 1,940 acres in tobacco, for a total of just over 2,231 acres in the island's major export crops. Meanwhile, the total acreage for the five subsistence crops (plantains, corn, rice, sweet potatoes, and yams) totaled well over twice the acreage in export crops at 56,968 acres.[52]

While there were four sugar *haciendas* in the Patillas region by 1840, very few of the town's inhabitants were part of the labor force on the big farms. As the *jornalero* laws came into effect in the 1840s, exemption from service required ownership of land, or being employed in a profession or trade, which ruled out all but 2 percent of the free colored population in Patillas.[53] Patillas demonstrates a community of free people of color living as subsistence farmers in a burgeoning sugar-producing region.

The availability of land made this subsistence lifestyle possible throughout Puerto Rico's history. Unoccupied lands were still plentiful in the first half of the nineteenth century, making labor control difficult. The expansion of the population and the rise of a substantial agricultural sector began pushing this population into the frontier interior of the island by the mid–nineteenth century. Even in the nineteenth century, the majority of Puerto Ricans lived in villages and small towns, most with fewer than 4,000 inhabitants. Over 70 percent of the population was illiterate, and few had marketable trades. In addition to subsistence farming, Puerto Rican peasants worked occasionally on the farms and *haciendas* of large landowners, moving from *hacienda* to *hacienda* with little regard to the needs of the landowners.

In the 1840s, sugar prices were declining, and *hacienda* owners needed to find ways to cut production costs. The cost of slaves rose 200 percent between the years 1820 and 1850; ending the reliance on an expensive slave labor force seemed a good option.[54] *Hacienda* owners complained that the work of the free laborers was more costly than the work of slaves because they were so difficult to control.[55] It wasn't until the middle of the nineteenth century that strict laws would be designed to help curtail what planters considered as a vagrancy problem. The Puerto Rican government did little before that to regulate free laborers. The 1840s, however, saw a rise in efforts to corral the island's independent work force through anti-vagrancy laws and other coercive means. The most drastic result of this was the General Law for Day Workers or the *Ley General de Jornaleros*, promulgated by Governor Juan de la Pezuela in 1849. The basic purpose of the law was to help alleviate the structural difficulties faced by the struggling sugar industry.[56] The preceding stories of people and towns illustrate interactions of free people of color, both immigrant and native, with each other and with whites in their communities. Each town is a different piece of the fabric, yet when the quilt is put together, we have a unique view of the social construction of the island's opening years of the nineteenth century. How whites and blacks interacted, how free people of color fit into the society at large, and how free people of color constructed their daily lives, are told through different stories in different towns throughout the island.

The majority of free people of color—in fact the majority of Puerto Rico's population—did not live in the large urban capital of San Juan. They lived in smaller, less urban municipalities scattered around the island. The interactions between whites and blacks appear in a different light when viewed beyond the cramped quarters of the walled capital. Out among the small towns and villages of the island, Puerto Ricans regarded themselves as a community that valued social rank over racial rank. Puerto Rico's unique demographics allowed its inhabitants the opportunity to approach race relations differently. The island's free people of color and poor whites were not deeply divided by economic or social standards. Economically, free people of color and poor whites were the numerical majority on the island. Socially, free people of color and whites found a way to coexist without the degree of fear or antagonism found elsewhere in the region.

The records highlight varying issues regarding daily life in early nineteenth-century Puerto Rico. Racial structure within households, women's issues, labor distribution in a community, and color classification and social status were all part of the daily struggle to survive. In the nineteenth century, Puerto Rico's free people of color and whites developed a society that revolved around survival and community.

Notes

1. Fernando Pico. "Esclavos, cimarrones, y negros libres en Río Piedras, 1774–1873." *Anuario De Estudios Americanos* (1986).

2. Ben Vinson, *Bearing arms for his majesty: The free-colored militia in colonial Mexico* (Stanford, CA: Stanford University Press, 2003); Adriana Naveda Chávez-Hita, *Esclavos negros en las haciendas azucareras de Córdoba, Veracruz, 1690–1830* (Xalapa, Ver., México: Universidad Veracruzana, Centro de Investigaciones Históricas, 1987); Verena Martínez-Alier, *Marriage, Class, and Colour in Nineteenth-Century Cuba: A Study of Racial Attitudes and Sexual Values in a Slave Society* (London: Cambridge University Press, 1974); Camillia Cowling, "'As a slave woman and as a mother': women and the abolition of slavery in Havana and Rio de Janeiro," *Social History* 36, no. 3 (2011): 294–311; María de los Ángeles Meriño Fuentes and Aisnara Perera Díaz, "Matrimonio y familia en el ingenio, una utopía posible. Cuba (1825–1886)." *Caribbean Studies* 3, no. 1 (Jan 2006): 201–37; Michele Reid-Vazquez, *The Year of the Lash: Free People of Color in Cuba and the Nineteenth-century Atlantic World* (Athens: University of Georgia Press, 2011); Christine Hünefeldt, *Paying the Price of Freedom: Family and Labor Among Lima's Slaves, 1800–1854* (Berkeley: University of California Press, 1995); María Elena Martínez, "The Black Blood of New Spain: Limpieza De Sangre, Racial Violence, and Gendered Power in Early Colonial Mexico," *The William and Mary Quarterly* 61, no. 3 (2004): 479–520.

3. Jay Kinsbruner, "Caste and Capitalism in the Caribbean: Residential Pattern and House Ownership Among the Free People of Color of San Juan, Puerto Rico, 1823–1846." *Hispanic American Historical Review* 70.3 (1990); Jorge L. Chinea, "Race, Colonial Exploitation and West Indian Immigration in Nineteenth-Century Puerto Rico, 1800–1860." *The Americas* 54.4(1996): 495–520; Teresita Martinez Vergene, *Capitalism in Colonial Puerto Rico: Central San Vicente in the Late Nineteenth Century* (Gainesville: University Press of Florida, 1992).

4. Benjamín Nistal-Moret, *Esclavos prófugos y cimarrones: Puerto Rico, 1770–1870* (Río Piedras: Editorial de la Universidad de Puerto Rico, 1984); Francisco A. Scarano, *Sugar and Slavery in Puerto Rico: The Plantation Economy in Ponce, 1800–1850* (Madison: University of Wisconsin Press, 1984); Guillermo A. Baralt, *Esclavos Rebeldes: Conspiraciones y sublevaciones de esclavos en Puerto Rico, 1795–1873* (Río Piedras: Ediciones Huracán, 1982).

5. Adapted from David W. Cohen and Jack P. Greene, *Neither Slave nor Free: The Freedman of African Descent in Slave Societies of the New World* (Baltimore: The Johns Hopkins University Press, 1972), 335–39.

6. Cohen and Greene, *Neither Slave nor Free*, 335–39.

7. Ibid., 338.

8. Cayetano Coll y Toste. *Boletín Histórico de Puerto Rico*. Vol. 9. 14 vols. (San Juan: Tipografía Cantero Fernández, 1914–1927), 72–73.

9. Fondo Gobernadores Españoles de Puerto Rico [FGEPR], Political and Civil Affairs, caja 11; FGEPR, Visitas 1818–1824.

10. FGEPR, Political and Civil Affairs, caja 15; Cayetano Coll y Toste. *Boletín Histórico de Puerto Rico*. Vol. 9. 14 vols. (San Juan: Tipografía Cantero Fernández, 1914–1927), 284.

11. FGEPR, Political and Civil Affairs, Censo y Riqueza, Caja 191; Jalil Sued Badillo and Ángel López Cantos, *Puerto Rico negro*. (Río Piedras: Editorial Cultural, 1986), 257–58.

12. FGEPR, Political and Civil Affairs, caja 11 – 13; David W. Cohen and Jack P. Greene. *Neither Slave nor Free: The Freedman of African Descent in Slave Societies of the New World*. (Baltimore: The Johns Hopkins University Press, 1972).

13. Dr. Hall's assertion was ground-breaking scholarship in the early 1970s and directed scholarship on free black politics and social movements for subsequent decades. Scholars such as David Patrick Geggus and Laurent DuBois have further developed her theories in their studies on revolutionary San Domingue. Gwendolyn Midlo Hall, "Saint Domingue," in *Neither Slave nor Free: The Freedman of African Descent in Slave Societies of the New World*, ed. David W. Cohen and Jack P. Greene. (Baltimore: The Johns Hopkins University Press, 1972); Laurent Dubois and John D. Garrigus, *Slave Revolution in the Caribbean, 1789–1804: A Brief History with Documents* (Basingstoke: Palgrave Macmillan, 2006); David Barry Gaspar and David Patrick Geggus, *A Turbulent Time: The French Revolution and the Greater Caribbean*. Bloomington: Indiana University Press, 1997).

14. Gad Heuman, "The Social Structure of the Slave Societies in the Caribbean," in *The Slave Societies of the Caribbean* ed. Franklin Knight. Vol. 3. (UNESCO Publication, 1997).

15. William Claypole and John Robottom, *Book One: Foundations* (London: Longman Group Limited, 1989), 115–16.

16. N. A. T. Hall, "Slave Laws of the Danish Virgin Islands in the Later Eighteenth Century," in *Comparative Perspectives on Slavery in New World Plantation Societies*, ed. Arthur Tuden and Vera Rubin (New York: New York Academy of Sciences, 1977); Edward Cox, *Free Coloreds in the Slave Societies of St. Kitts and Grenada, 1763–1833* (Knoxville: University of Tennessee Press, 1984).

17. Works on free people of color in slave societies for the English-speaking Caribbean region include: Ira Berlin, *Slaves Without Masters: The Free Negro in the Antebellum South* (New York: Oxford University Press, 1974); Sheena Boa, "Urban Free Black and Coloured Women: Jamaica, 1760–1834," *Jamaican Historical Review* 18(1993): 1–6; Carl Campbell, "Rise of Free Colored Plantocracy in Trinidad, 1783–1813," *Bolentín de estudios latino-americanos y del Caribe* 29(1980): 35–53; Mavis C. Campbell, *The Maroons of Jamaica, 1655–1796* (Trenton: Africa World Press, Inc., 1990); Lambros

Comitas and David Lowenthal, *Slaves, Free Men, and Citizens: West Indian Perspectives* (New York: Anchor, 1973); Edward Cox, *Free Coloreds in the Slave Societies of St. Kitts and Grenada, 1763–1833* (Knoxville: University of Tennessee Press, 1984); Laura Forner, "The Free People of Color in Louisiana and St. Domingue: A Comparative Portrait of Two Three-Caste Slave Societies," *Journal of Social History* 3.4 (1970): 407–30; John Hope Franklin, *The Free Negro in North Carolina, 1790–1860* (Chapel Hill: University of North Carolina Press, 1943); Jerome S. Handler, *Unappropriated People: Freedmen in the Slave Society of Barbados* (Baltimore: The Johns Hopkins University Press, 1974); Gad Heuman, "The Social Structure of the Slave Societies in the Caribbean," in *The Slave Societies of the Caribbean*, ed. Franklin Knight. Vol. 3. (UNESCO Publication, 1997); Gad J. Heuman, *Between Black and White: Race, Politics, and the Free Coloreds in Jamaica, 1792–1865* (Westport, CT: Greenwood Press, 1981); Peter H. Wood, *Black Majority: Negroes in Colonial South Carolina from 1670 Through the Stono Rebellion* (New York: Norton, 1975).

Works on the Francophone Caribbean include: Carolyn E. Fick, *The Making of Haiti: The Saint Domingue Revolution From Below* (Knoxville: University of Tennessee Press, 1990); Laura Forner, "The Free People of Color in Louisiana and St. Domingue: A Comparative Portrait of Two Three-Caste Slave Societies," *Journal of Social History* 3.4 (1970): 407–30; John D. Garrigus and Christopher Morris, *Assumed Identities the Meanings of Race in the Atlantic World* (College Station: Published for the University of Texas at Arlington by Texas A & M University Press, 2010); Kimberly S. Hanger, *Bounded Lives, Bounded Places: Free Black Society in Colonial New Orleans, 1769–1803* (Durham, NC: Duke University Press, 1997); Jane Landers, *Atlantic Creoles in the Age of Revolutions* (Cambridge: Harvard University Press, 2010).

Brazil is covered in: George Reid Andrews, *Blacks and Whites in São Paulo, Brazil, 1888–1988* (Madison: University of Wisconsin Press, 1991); Carl Degler, *Neither Black nor White: Slavery and Race Relations in Brazil and the United States* (Madison: University of Wisconsin Press, 1971); Herbert S. Klein, "The Colored Freedmen in Brazilian Slave Society," *Journal of Social History* 3.1 (1969): 31–45; Katia M. de Queiros Mattoso, "Slave, Free, and Freed Family Structures in Nineteenth Century Salvador Bahia," *Luso-Brazilian Review* 25.1 (1988): 75–84.

And a sampling of works on free people of color in the Spanish Americas includes: Herman L. Bennett, *Colonial Blackness: A History of Afro-Mexico* (Bloomington: Indiana University Press, 2009); Frederick Bowser, *The African Slave in Colonial Peru, 1524–1650* (Redwood City, CA: Stanford University Press, 1974); Franklin J. Franco, *Los negros, los mulatos y la nación dominican* (Santo Domingo, República Dominicana: Editora Manatí, 2003); Christine Hünefeldt, *Paying the Price of Freedom: Family and Labor Among Lima's Slaves, 1800–1854* (Berkeley: University of California Press, 1994); Lyman L. Johnson, "Manumission in Colonial Buenos Aires, 1776–1810," *Hispanic American Historical Review* 59.2 (1979): 258–79; Jay Kinsbruner, *Not of Pure*

Blood: The Free People of Color and Racial Prejudice in Nineteenth-Century Puerto Rico (Durham, NC: Duke University Press, 1996); Jane Landers, *Atlantic Creoles in the Age of Revolutions* (Cambridge: Harvard University Press, 2010); Suzanne Lebsock, *The Free Women of Petersburg: Status and Culture in a Southern Town* (New York: Norton, 1985); Magnus Mörner, *Race Mixture in the History of Latin America* (Boston: Little, Brown, 1967); Fernando Pico, "Esclavos, cimarrones, y negros libres en Río Piedras, 1774–1873," *Anuario De Estudios Americanos* (1986): 1–24; Michele Reid-Vazquez, *The Year of the Lash: Free People of Color in Cuba and the Nineteenth-century Atlantic World* (Athens: University of Georgia Press, 2011).

18. Arnold A. Sio, "Marginality and Free Coloured Identity in Caribbean Slave Society," in *Caribbean Slave Society and Economy,* ed. Hilary Beckles and Verene A. Shepherd (New York: New Press, 1991).

19. Outlined in chapter two, the *Bando Contra la Raza Africana* (*Proclamation against the African Race*) was promulgated by Governor Juan Prim y Prats at the end of May 1848 as a measure to control both the free and enslaved black populations on the island. Both Prim y Prats and the Proclamation were short-lived on the island, and by November 1848, both were a bitter memory to the Puerto Rican people.

20. FGEPR, Political and Civil Affairs, Censo y Riqueza, 1812–1828; Archivo Historico Nacional [AHN]. Madrid. Ultramar 5103, exp. 64, 3 January 1874 at CIH, UPR, roll 164, n.d.

21. In the 1850s, only one in eleven Puerto Ricans was literate. The first printing press was brought to the island in the first decade of the nineteenth century. Arturo Morales Carrión, *Puerto Rico: A Political and Cultural History* (New York: W. W. Norton & Company, 1983), 130.

22. FGEPR, Political and Civil Affairs, Censo y Riqueza, 1812–1828; FGEPR, Municipalities, Aguadilla, n.d.

23. FGEPR, Municipalities, Aguadilla, n.d.; FGEPR Emigrados 1815–1837, caja 54; FGEPR, Extranjeros 1807–1845; FGEPR, Consules y Gobiernos, Extranjeros. Curaçao, 1762–1838.

24. FGEPR, Municipalities, Aguadilla, n.d.; FGEPR, Escalvos -- Negros Libertos. 1799–1825.

25. FGEPR, Municipalities, Aguadilla, n.d.; FGEPR, Political and Civil Affairs. Emigrados. 1815–1837.

26. FGEPR, Consules y Gobiernos Extranjeros. Costa Firme. 1821–1835.

27. FGEPR, Municipalities. Añasco. n.d.

28. FGEPR, Consules y Gobiernos Extranjeros. Costa Firme. 1821–1835; FGEPR, Visitas, 1824.

29. FGEPR, Visitas, 1824; Consules y Gobiernos Extranjeros. Caracas. 1796–1821.

30. Kinsbruner, *Not of Pure Blood*, 1996.

31. Ibid.

32. FGEPR, Municipalities, Añasco, n.d.

33. Félix Matos-Rodríguez, *Women and Urban Change in San Juan, Puerto Rico, 1820–1868* (Gainesville: University of Florida Press, 1999).

34. FGEPR, Municipalities, Aguadilla, n.d.

35. FGEPR, Municipalities, Rincón, n.d.

36. FGEPR, Municipalities, Toa Alta, n.d.   ·

37. AHN. Madrid. Ultramar 5103, exp. 64, 3 January 1874 at CIH, UPR, roll 164, n.d.

38. FGEPR, Municipalities, Toa Alta, n.d.

39. Ibid.

40. AHN. Madrid. Ultramar 5103, exp. 64, 3 January 1874 at CIH, UPR, roll 164, n.d. FGEPR, Justicia, 1796–1816).

41. FGEPR, Justicia, 1817–1822.

42. Ibid.

43. *Actas Del Cabildo De San Juan De Bautista De Puerto Rico 1730–1821.* Vols. 1–18. (San Juan: Municipio de San Juan, 1968–1970).

44. Flinter contended that the planters on the island were so benevolent that their slaves were much better off than the free laborers of Europe. He also implied that the increase and the slave population on the island was due to natural reproduction rather than recent importations. George D. Flinter, *An Account of the Present State of the Island of Puerto Rico. Comprising Numerous Original Facts and Documents Illustrative of the State of Commerce and Agriculture, and of the Condition, Moral and Physical, of the Various Classes of the Population in That Island, as Compared With the Colonies of Other European Powers; Demonstrating the Superiority of the Spanish Slave Code, – the Great Advantages of Free Over Slave Labor, &c.* (London: Longman, Rees, Orme, Brown, Green, and Longman, 1834).

45. Flinter, *Present State of the Island*, 1832.

46. Baralt, *Esclavos Rebeldes*, 1982; Nistal-Moret, *Escalvos prófugos*, 1984.

47. Andrés Ramos Mattei, *Azucar y esclavitud.* (San Juan: Ediciones Huracán, 1982); Francisco A. Scarano, *Puerto Rico: cinco siglos de historia* (San Juan: McGraw-Hill, 1993).

48. Morales Carrión, *Auge y decadencia*, 134–35.

49. FGEPR, Municipalities, Patillas, n.d.

50. Ibid.

51. Ibid.

52. Morales Carrión, *Auge y decadencia*, 134–35.

53. The Jornalero Laws of 1849 forced all landless Puerto Ricans to register with governmental authorities, secure work on the farms of large landowners, and to carry *libretos* – books noting employment conditions, work records, and behavior. *Actas Del Cabildo*, 1968–1970.

54. Labor Gómez Acevedo, *Organización y reglamentación del trabajo en el Puerto Rico del siglo XIX (propietarios y jornaleros)* (San Juan: Instituto de Cultura Puertorriqueña, 1970).

55. Morales Carrión, *Auge y decadencia*, 134–35.

56. The *Jornalero* law sits just outside the timeframe of this project but does merit an explanation. The law created a new civil category within the census *jornalero*, which was composed of any citizen who could not prove land ownership or some professional skill, regardless of race. Those classified as *jornaleros* were forced to seek employment on legally titled farms where employers recorded work schedules, behavior, and movement in small passbooks called *libretas*. These booklets were to be carried at all times by the *jornalero*. For the *hacienda* owner, this seemed the perfect solution to labor woes and population control. For the Puerto Rican peasant, used to controlling his own time and maneuverings, this was the ultimate in state interference and coerciveness.

Chapter Four

Til Death Do Us Part: Engagement, Elopement, Marriage, and Widowhood

Eighteenth- and nineteenth-century free women of color in the Atlantic World played a significant role in the development of the cultures and societies we know today, but few scholars have thus far acknowledged the contributions of these women. Groundbreaking work such as *More than Chattel: Black Women and Slavery in the Americas*, edited by David Barry Gaspar and Darlene Clark Hine, or *The Bondwoman's Narrative*, by Hannah Craft and edited by Henry Louis Gates, Jr., certainly begin to answer the question concerning how slavery touched the lives of black women in the Atlantic World. "Til Death Do Us Part" takes the inquiry one step further and asks what *freedom* meant to black women. This chapter broadens the scope from the usual sphere of the antebellum United States, and seeks to include the Spanish Caribbean in the discussion of how black women, and especially free black women, were affected during this era.

Examining the personal and interpersonal relationships of nineteenth-century Puerto Rican women of color humanizes the archival records. Scholarship on slavery in the Atlantic World has expanded in recent years, yet the study of free people of color within the world of slavery is still an oft-overlooked subject. The growing interest in the history of black women in slavery benefits from a study of women who were not enslaved. This chapter explores how place of origin affected personal perceptions of space, color, or class; how women and people of color construct identity; what it meant to be a woman of color in nineteenth-century Puerto Rico; and what it meant to be black and free in a slave society.

Laws and Life in the Spanish World

Strict laws governing marriage were laid out by the Spanish Crown in the late eighteenth century and amplified at the beginning of the nineteenth century.[1] They gave parents recourse to prevent their dependents from entering into undesirable marriages to partners of lower social, economic, or racial backgrounds. The Royal Decree of April 10, 1803, building on earlier enactments, was the most specific and far-reaching. The purpose of this governmental incursion into the households of the Spanish colonies was to prevent unwanted marriages to partners who were deemed of a lower social class or of a different race.[2]

Until 1803, individual parents exercised control over choice of spouse in Spain's New World colonies. The civil authorities could only intervene if sons or daughters challenged parental dissent.[3] Persistent ambiguities relating to the interracial marriage policy in the western colonies caused the matter to be submitted to the Council of the Indies. On October 15, 1805, the Council issued a Royal Decree on marriages between persons of known nobility with members of the castes of *negro* and *mulato*.[4] The Audiencia of Puerto Principe in Cuba issued an edict reiterating the October 1805 Decree on July 9, 1806. Finally, on December 18, 1810, the Viceroy of Mexico issued an edict emphatically stating that this decree must be understood to apply to "the persons of known nobility *or* known purity of blood." [emphasis mine] While this was primarily a document aimed at white colonial families with noble European lineage, non-noble whites and free people of color used it as a measure of status within their own social milieus.

By prohibiting men under age twenty-five and women under age twenty-three from marrying without consent, the Decree allowed parents the right to approve of, and intervene in, the marriages of their children.[5] The Decree, and all its subsequent forms, did not go unchallenged at the local level. Citizens throughout the Spanish Americas challenged the Decree through various means, including simply ignoring its edicts or actively seeking government channels by which to circumvent the law. Petitions directed through a regional *alcalde* (magistrate, mayor) were the main form of challenge found in early nineteenth-century Puerto Rico.

Two underage orphans, María Catalina Pérez, a white woman from the Canary Islands, and Manuel de Jesús, a *moreno* from Puerto Rico, had neither family nor relatives in Puerto Rico who could have contested their marriage, so the *alcalde* of Río Piedras offered official objections. In 1820, María formally issued a response to the *alcalde* for the right to marry Manuel. She argued that the government had no jurisdiction in the matter, since the parents of both parties were deceased. María, a recent immigrant, was over the age of twenty-three, which legally freed her to marry without familial consent. Another factor in her petition emphasized that after verbally contracting a marriage with Manuel, she had three children by him. Her petition stated that she had no problem with Manuel "not being of equal blood"; however, she was quite content that he was willing to marry her in her orphaned state.[6]

Petitions filed by the *alcalde* on behalf of deceased parents were rare. María's response was even more rare, being that it was a counter-petition by a female plaintiff. Unlike most Puerto Ricans of either sex, María was literate. She apparently came from a family that valued education and personal freedom, and her petitions suggest that her parents would have accepted her judgment, as well as embraced Manuel as their future son-in-law.[7] María was determined to marry Manuel, despite their "difference of color," and used all available resources to make her case. Manuel's voice, heard through María's testimony, is one of loyalty and earnestness. He wanted to stand by his pledge of marriage and allow his children to be legitimized through marriage.[8]

Marriage also was used as a method by which families could assert their power and position in the Puerto Rican social hierarchy. Since the 1803 royal decree allowed parents the right to intervene in the marriage plans of their children, issues of color between potential partners became a factor by which families battled for social supremacy. Color was sometimes a minor issue that had little or no bearing on the proceedings. Other times, however, color was a badge of honor used to clarify and solidify a family's social standing.

A major reason for parental objection was the concept of inequality of color and status.[9] The mobility aspirations of the various social levels often came into conflict when the children desired marriage to socially unequal partners. The differences in the social structure of the free colored community were reflected in the reasons for parental dissent to marriage. Generally, parental objection was prompted by differences in color and in status. The basic attitude of parents was that in choosing a spouse, one should endeavor to "advance instead of regress."[10] The term "advance" was used in relation to one's color, which was defined by the "cleansing" one's family tree of "impure bloodlines" and in reference to one's distance from slavery. The further removed from slavery, the greater the chances of ascending the social ladder. In one case, María José Betancourt objected to her brother, "blinded and obscured by an amorous passion," contracting a marriage to a woman from the *"parda* class" who was a "descendent of slaves on both sides." The Betancourt family had papers proving their pure Spanish lineage, and "no one in the family could lend their consent" to the brother who "unjustly bonded himself to an *obscure* person."[11] [emphasis mine]

Differences more subtle than that were perceived as an obstacle to marriage. The son of two fourth-degree *pardo* parents (quadroons; one-quarter black) aroused his father's wrath when he attempted to marry a *parda* on both sides (both parents were *mulatos*). The father opposed the marriage because of the "conspicuous inequality" between the two. It was not her complexion but her bloodline; despite successive generations of cross-racial unions, she was still conspicuously "darker" than that of her suitor.[12] The father contested that his son should—more than simply preserve past gains—endeavor to "advance the family."[13]

In this case of *pardo* family against *pardo* family, it was the *perception* of inequality due to "unequal" blood that stood in the way of the marriage union. The son of the contesting family was at least three generations removed on either side from any "negro bloodlines." The opposition was to a bride who was only two generations removed. The Betancourt family felt it was important to maintain or "improve" their blood lines in an effort to "cleanse" the family tree.

Blood played an important role in marriage petitions. Most often it was not the skin color, but the perceived threat to "bloodlines" that determined marriage compatibility. "Clean origin" was valued.[14] Blood was the important conduit of family heritage and told of social, cultural, and moral status. "Unequal blood" could stem from parents who had committed a sin against the church, broken government edicts or laws, or had African or Indian ancestry. Illegitimacy was another factor that could taint the "blood" of a perspective mate. But "not equal in blood" or "impure blood," in most petitions covered in this work, was a reference to African or slave ancestry.

Occasionally, the principles of the 1803 decree were indirectly implied in disparaging letters sent back and forth between families, with each claiming the other was concealing their black relatives. Don Apolinario López wanted to marry María San Diego de Castro in 1822. María was the daughter of a highly respected master silversmith from Caguas. At first, María's father opposed the marriage on the grounds that Sr. López was not a respectable enough candidate for his daughter, and that his intentions toward his daughter were not perceived to be honest. The López family countered with a petition stating that they opposed the marriage since it was well known that María's maternal side of the family had *pardo* blood and presented Maria's official birth certificate, which recorded her as being *parda*.[15] Other letters followed in which both the López family and the Castro family attempted to identify black ancestry on each other's family trees.[16] Interestingly, both María's father and her suitor were white. Her father objected because he felt Apolinario made a pledge to María without any intention of marrying his daughter.

The perceived relationship between respect, honor, and color was a common theme throughout the early nineteenth century, and all these variables were important elements of marriage petitions. Comparisons of cross-racial versus same-race marriages did not show much disparity between the two issues. Color tended not to be the central factor for refusing marriage; instead issues of honor, social standing, and family respectability were given the most weight. "Inequality of blood" was a frequently utilized argument, characterized by the Spanish phrase *"por su calidad de pardo,"* to contest marriage proposals. It is interesting to note that this was an argument often used by *pardos* against *pardos*.

The families of Luís de Jesús and Petrona Andújar provide an example of one free family of color opposing another based primarily on perceived "inequality of blood." Petrona's relatives were worried because Luís had been characterized as a "man of questionable conduct," and they soon discovered that he was one-quarter *pardo*. Since Luís had tried to suppress this information, the Andújar family used the discovery as part of their argument against his character. The Jesús family, who admitted to being *pardo*, quickly revealed that when Petrona was born, her mother was still a slave.[17] Even though her father was a free *pardo* and her mother was eventually freed, the Jesús family argued that Petrona was unsuitable for their son since she was "not equal in blood" to Luís.

In the end the Andújar family won the battle, and Petrona and Luís were not allowed to marry. The *alcalde* ruled that Luís was under the age of twenty-one, did not make enough money at his *fumacero* (cigar-rolling) job to support Petrona, and was not a trustworthy young man since he was prone to infidelities.[18] Here it becomes obvious through the argument of the *alcalde's* ruling that, while color and social standing based on color were important parts of the development of character and acceptability, they were not all-encompassing, nor were they all-important factors.

Not admitting to *pardo* bloodlines cost Luís his marriage to Petrona, yet *pardo* blood was not a hindrance in this proposal. It was his character and lack of responsibility that were in question. Petrona's family wanted her to be monetarily and emotionally supported. They also did not want their family name to be connected with a social outcast. Translations and analysis are complex when dealing with perceived "inequality of blood." Careful analysis of notions of color and color acceptance within other known areas of study are needed. Neither the example of the British islands or the United States provides useful comparisons. Cuba and Brazil were perhaps the closest examples to Puerto Rico, yet even they lacked the broad acceptance of free people of color in their societies. Certainly, Puerto Rico was not a utopia, and race did play a role in everyday interactions; however, race and color did not tend to confine a person to a social caste. Puerto Rican free people of color continually existed outside what the majority of Caribbeanists and Americanists would consider their proper space.[19]

In the eyes of some parents, in some individual cases, factors other than differences in color and legal status made a marriage undesirable. As in the case of Petrona and Luís, objection was taken to the suitor's economic standing, moral reputation, unfaithfulness, and proven virtue. There is one petition where the candidate is said to be a "drunkard" and another one a "loose, thievish and dissolute *moreno*." There were various other petitions, including one where a worried father described the perils of marrying a fallen woman.[20]

A prominent *pardo* family from San German hired an investigator in 1836 to search the fuzzy background of Doña María del Carmén González, the woman their son, Don Alonzo Ramírez, intended to marry. Doña María was found to be "not a person who came from a good family ... and her antecedents on her mother's side had been slaves." They also uncovered the fact that she had changed her surname from Sales to González, in an attempt to disassociate herself from her own family and pass herself off as coming from a more prominent family. While her father had been a soldier from Cataluna, her Puerto Rican mother was "reputed to be a *mulata*."[21] Don Alonzo had been unaware of the questionable heritage of his intended. His family made it clear that they would not have their lineage obscured by such an impostor.[22]

Once again, it is the *concealment* of heritage that makes the issue one of character rather than of race. The Ramírez family was concerned about their standing in the community. The members of the Ramírez family are respected in San German society, which is noted through the use of honorific titles (*don* and *doña*). A social imposter such as María del Carmén could be perceived as dangerous to their social standing. Her name change, the "reputedly *mulata*" mother, hints of illegitimacy, and issues of character and respectability made the match untenable for the Ramírez family.

Occasionally, the parents objected to a cross-racial marriage on the grounds that the woman was disreputable. One man felt he could not agree to his brother's choice because she was a "scandalous *parda*" who had lived in concubinage with his brother for seven years while her husband was still alive. He thought this was reason enough to "deny his consent for such an unequal monstrous marriage." One wonders whether the accent here was on "scandalous" or "*parda*."[23]

Relative social status among free people of color was dependent on color and legal status. Individual performance could enhance an individual's status, but advancement on this scale was checked to some degree by the circumstances of birth. In the final analysis, it was an individual's status with regard to slavery that mattered. The greater the removal from slavery, the more social worth a person had. Skin color was a means to assess this status. *Pardos* occupied a higher place on the social ladder, not only because of their phenotypical approximation to the whites, but more importantly, because they were likely to be genealogically and socially further removed from slavery.

Among free people of color, a very general aspiration was to get as far away from slavery as possible. Most whites viewed the partial slave heritage of *pardos* with a sense of superiority; in turn, *pardos* themselves often applied a similar disdain to their free colored peers. In Puerto Rico, slavery never reached the proportions it did on its sister island of Cuba, or any other Caribbean island. The racial dynamics were different because of this unique situation. Regardless of the small number of slaves and the relative ease by which slaves could be manumitted in early nineteenth-century Puerto Rico, slavery was still viewed as a deeply undesirable social condition.

Admittedly, the number of cases of parental objection to marriage among free people of color that were taken to the authorities was small compared to the size and the number of marriages of the free colored population. It could be argued that relatively few parents really cared whether or not the marriages of their children were color- or status-endogamous.

Elopement in early nineteenth-century Puerto Rico was seen as a form of challenge to family honor, social prestige, and feminine virtue. Faced with the prospect of a daughter running away secretly to marry without parental consent, a family had three main courses of action, each of which is discussed respectively. If the challenger was equal in status to the family, then marriage was an adequate solution. If the suitor was inferior in status, the appropriate action was a criminal conviction on charges of abduction and/or seduction. If the suitor was superior in status, then a third alternative presented itself: the family might be required to put up with the dishonor imposed on their family and daughter.[24]

When families objected to a match, they often placed obstacles in the path of the young couple, which, in turn, could in fact result in elopement. The aim of this drastic step was to reverse the attitude of the objecting parents, and, in the best-case scenario, to create a situation that would compel the parents to actively promote the marriage. The sequence of events was usually that the girl disappeared for a few days and the relationship was consummated. The suitor then gave himself up, or the police found the couple.[25] The essential point is that the girl had lost her virtue and her honor. The shame brought on their daughter would presumably cause parents to reverse their course and assent to the legal union. The rationale was that initially the family honor was thought to be damaged by an unsuitable pairing, but in the face of the daughter's shame, it was precisely the family honor that now demanded the marriage.

María Antonia Crespo was in her kitchen the night of January 23, 1820. Her suitor, Don Antonio Lorenzo de Acevedo, stopped by for refreshments; thereafter, the two of them left for Mayagüez, without her parents' approval. Once at the town church, Don Antonio presented María Antonia to the priest and asked that they be married. Unfortunately for this couple, the priest immediately sent for the girl's father and suggested to the couple that they wait a little more patiently for the magistrate's ruling. María was a *parda* and Don Antonio was white. They needed special dispensation to marry, because María's father had placed a petition with the magistrate opposing the union due to his daughter's young age.[26]

After the attempted elopement, both fathers further petitioned the magistrate against the marriage. Don Antonio Crespo, María's father, continued to object that his daughter was still too young. He also objected because the suitor had shown a "blatant disregard for the desires" of the Crespo family by whisking his daughter away without consent. The suitor's father "highly objected" because of the "enormous difference" in their colors and also their young age. The fact that the two ran off "without a doubt was an insult to the honest" process by which the two families had been trying to work out their differences.[27]

Children utilized elopement to circumvent parental control. Parents would initially attempt to settle the matter outside the courts. If that did not work, the case would go before the magistrate. The reasons that induced parents to oppose a given marriage usually reflected their desire to preserve family honor in terms of social status. For free people of color, family, and community honor were closely related to individual honor. Dishonorable conduct on the part of one free person of color directly affected the prestige of all.

The high status given to female honor within the free colored community provided a suitable mechanism to control marriage. Family integrity was preserved through the protection of the moral integrity of the women. It was through women that family attributes were transmitted from generation to generation. Men fulfilled oversaw the socially acceptable transfer of these attributes through their role as guardians of the virtue and honor of their family women. In turn, by protecting the virtue of its women, the free colored community protected its social status.[28]

Elopement was a procedure daughters utilized to force parents to allow them to live with their chosen mates out of wedlock. The suitor would take the girl away, and they would set up house together, "as if they were already married," on the understanding that they *would* marry once his financial status improved.[29] María Catalina and her suitor, Manuel, presumably opted for this sort of arrangement.[30] Often, parents would show outrage initially, but acquiesce soon after, when it was revealed their relationships began in much the same manner. Rarely were these types of cases brought to court. This is understandable because the suitor was thought to be acting in good faith, and the girl's parents trusted him to marry her when his circumstances allowed. If the marriage occurred, there was no reason for parental or official intervention.

It appears non-church-sanctioned unions such as María Catalina and Manuel's did receive a certain amount of social recognition. Marriage was very much a symbol of status. For marriage to hold any social meaning, it demanded a measure of public display and ritual, which, in turn, demanded a sizable outlay of money. It was probably this major expenditure that prevented some couples from immediately entering into a legal union.[31] When coupled with a lack of property or status, these non-church-sanctioned unions seemed to be a viable option to a great many poor Puerto Ricans, both white and free colored.

But the non-sanctioned unions were not a viable option for those who held status or were seeking to raise their status. Legal unions brought honor to families and respect to the individuals involved, regardless of color. For free people of color, legal unions meant an added boost to the social image they were trying to portray of moral, honorable, and respectable people, the kind one would want one's offspring to marry.

Puerto Rican free people of color, as with most Spanish colonials, highly valued female honor. Documents spoke of the "honor" that had been "lost" by daughters at the hands of unsavory men and demanded their honor be "saved" or "repaired." The respectability and modesty of the girls were emphasized in petitions to highlight the "wrongs" done to the daughters and to their families.[32]

In 1820, a soldier pledged his love to Juana de Torres. He promised her he would marry her and that "their love would know no end." When Juana became pregnant, the soldier denounced her, broke the engagement, and transferred out of town. Juana's father wrote to the magistrate begging him to force the soldier to return, stand by his pledge of marriage, and "return honor" to his daughter. He asked the magistrate to ignore the fact that Juana was *parda* and the soldier was white and to rule on the "side of what is right and honorable" as is befitting a "soldier of the Crown."[33]

Of course, sometimes the girl could use the procedure to trap a young man into marriage. Antonia de la Cruz, a *morena*, accused her suitor, also a *moreno*, of pledging marriage and leaving her when she became pregnant. The accused countered, that if this was true, Antonia had yet to produce an offspring even though the accusation occurred almost 18 months previously. While he admitted to asking for her hand and then retracting his pledge, he swore that she was not pregnant when he left. In fact, he claimed that he had discovered that she was not a virgin, which was the reason why he broke off the engagement. He wished to be exonerated of any "crime that he has been accused."[34]

As long as the social distance between families and candidates remained within acceptable boundaries, the social order was sustained and the girl's virtue remained intact. If the shame brought on the family was deemed greater than the shame brought on the daughter, the family honor was inviolable.

Verena Martínez-Alier argues that in order for honor and virtue to be effective as a device to safeguard social hierarchy, sometimes elopement had to succeed. If it were always allowed to succeed, the situation would ultimately bring about the very issues the boundaries were originally intending to prevent, namely, social equality. This brings about a fundamental contradiction. While social inequality demanded a high value placed on virginity, the risk of elopement implied freedom of choice in marriage, which in turn, was only available under conditions of social equality.[35] For free people of color, these issues of hierarchy and social equality were important in building cohesion and honor within their own community while gaining respectability in the eyes of the white community.

The practical reality of marriage, as it related to free people of color, affected the social structure in Puerto Rico. Women learned to negotiate the restraints placed on them by the patriarchal society and developed a space for themselves.

Marriage was often the most dignified role for a woman, if not her only one. Society was suspicious of single women, and a mother with children born out of wedlock was considered a threat to the marriages of others and to good Christian morals.[36] Even with the questionable morals and mores these women represented, their presence was a significant part of the social fabric of early nineteenth-century Puerto Rican towns. As we saw earlier in this chapter, women were often caught between the laws and reality when it came to choosing and settling down with a spouse. The church might sanction marriage, and the state might regulate marriage; however, the reality was that engagements disbanded, parents disapproved, lovers died or ran away, and women were left alone and single.

The majority of the single mothers were *labradoras*, a general term for peasant or farmer used in the Puerto Rican census, which is consistent with the general population of Puerto Rico in the early nineteenth century. Among the exceptions were fifty-year-old Ana la Rosa, a midwife, and twenty-four-year-old Rosalia González, a cook, both of Rincón.[37] Ana la Rosa's household included five children, ages two to twenty-seven. The range in the age of the children is probably an example of her grandchildren being counted as her own. More likely, the two children listed at ages two and six are the offspring of one or more of her three daughters, who were aged twenty, twenty-three, and twenty-seven years old.[38]

Often, for women the most direct route to respectability was widowhood. Widowhood could be a hindrance with no man to guard and provide for the woman and her children. Some women thrived by using their widow status for economic and social advancement. Women of color especially seemed to utilize this method of advancement.

Almost 12 percent of the free colored population in the northwestern town of Rincón was widowed. This included both male and female residents. When this number was combined with the single mothers, the proportion of single-parent households jumped to 26 percent of Rincón's total households. Single parents headed more than a quarter of the households in the free colored population of Rincón.[39] This might show a lack of social cohesion within the *pardo* community pointing to the kinds of family and social problems now associated with single-parent homes. The famous 1965 study by Daniel Patrick Moynihan, entitled *The Negro Family: The Case for National Action*, suggested that the desertion and illegitimacy rates associated with female-headed households were a product of a culture where the evil effects of slavery continued to be felt.[40] Critics of the study have suggested that there is no direct connection between having been raised in a matrifocal family and occurrences of illegitimacy, delinquency, or other social ills. Nor do critics believe that the experience of slavery in the past necessarily predisposes families to be poor and non-cohesive.[41]

Whether this phenomenon of households headed by single females was only prevalent in Rincón's free colored population is difficult to establish, since there is no way to compare it to the town's white population. The proportion of single-parent households was much higher than those in the white and *pardo* population of nearby Río Arríba, so Rincón might have been an anomaly.

Because nineteenth-century family units, family ties, and ancestry defined individual persons, marriage was important to the social fabric of free men and women of color in Puerto Rican society. For both white and colored women, marriage represented the only acceptable status they could achieve. It was considered their sole method of securing fortune, position, and respectability in society. But some Puerto Rican free women of color used the marriage process as a means of asserting their independence from dominant cultural ties. The study of marriage petitions filed through local magistrates that contested unequal unions, elopements, and attempted abductions demonstrates how the marriage process was often the glue that kept family and community ties together. Exploring patterns of recorded marriages in various regions of Puerto Rico shows how marriage was both shaped by and, in turn, shaped the community of free people of color.

Marriage petitions, elopement, marriage, and widowhood are distinct stages in the personal interaction of the Puerto Rican people. The study of extant documents offers a view of the commonalities between white and free colored neighbors. Interesting patterns and gender interactions that transcend racial categories are recognized. A glimpse of how Puerto Rican free people of color conceptualized their position in the nineteenth-century society is quite apparent. Familial ties were important; in the marriage petitions, family was an integral part of keeping family and community ties together. Elopement was a way of stepping outside the constraints of family and community. Marriage was both shaped by and, in turn, shaped the community of free people of color. Widowhood was a way to construct a new identity within the parameters of a highly gendered society. All the while, free people of color were negotiating their place within this evolving culture.

Notes

1. For more information on women and the institution of marriage in colonial Latin America see: Barbara Bush, *Slave Women in Caribbean Society, 1650–1838* (Bloomington: Indiana University Press, 1990; Verena Martínez-Alier, *Marriage, Class, and Colour in Nineteenth-Century Cuba: A Study of Racial Attitudes and Sexual Values in a Slave Society* (London: Cambridge University Press, 1974); Marietta Morrissey, *Slave Women in the New World: Gender Stratification in the Caribbean* (Lawrence: University of Kansas Press, 1989); Marysa Navarro, "Women in Pre-Columbian and Colonial Latin American," *Teaching Packets for Integrating Women's History into Courses on African, Asia, Latin America, the Caribbean, and the Middle East* (Bloomington, IN: Organization of American Historians, 1988); Patricia Seed, *To Love, Honor and Obey in Colonial Mexico: Conflicts Over Marriage Choice, 1574–1821* (Redwood City: Stanford University Press, 1988); Susan Socolow, "Acceptable Partners: Marriage Choice in Colonial Argentina, 1778–1810," in *Sexuality and Marriage in Colonial Latin America,* ed. Asunción Lavrin (Lincoln: University of Nebraska Press, 1989).

2. In 1776, the Spanish Crown enacted a *Pragmática Sanción* (Pragmatic Sanction) aimed at preventing unequal marriages resulting from the allegedly ill-understood freedom of marriage. Parental consent was made a formal requirement for those

under twenty-five years of age and/or living under parental tutelage. Parental dissent was deemed justified when it was thought the proposed marriage would "gravely offend family honor and jeopardize the integrity of the State." The 1776 Pragmatic Sanction affected mainly Spaniards living in Spain. In 1778, the revised Pragmatic Sanction extended to the overseas possessions in view of the "same or greater harm done there by such unequal marriages on account of their size and diversity of classes and castes of their inhabitants," and the "very severe damage done by the absolute and undisciplined freedom with which these passionate and incapable youngsters of both sexes betroth themselves." *Actas Del Cabildo De San Juan De Bautista De Puerto Rico 1730–1821."* Vols. 1–18. (San Juan: Municipio de San Juan, 1968–1970).

3. Martínez-Alier, *Marriage, Class, and Colour,* 12.

4. José María Zamora y Coronado, *Biblioteca de legislación ultramarina en forma de diccionario alfebeto* (Madrid, n.p., 1845).

5. Joaquín Rodríguez San Pedro, *Legislación ultramaria.* Vol. 5 (Madrid: Imprenta Manuel Minuesa, 1868), 514–15 and 518–19. For an excellent interpretation of the *real decreto* and its effect on free people of color in the Spanish Caribbean, see: Martínez-Alier, *Marriage, Class, and Colour,* 11–15.

6. Fondo Gobernadores Españoles de Puerto Rico [FGEPR], Ecclesiastic Affairs. Dispensas Matrimoniales. 1815–1822.

7. Ibid.

8. Spanish law allowed for children born out of wedlock to be considered of legitimate birth if their natural parents were to eventually become married. The children were then legitimized retroactively. This was not the case, however, if one parent was already married at the time of conception (cases of adultery) or if one of the parents was not the natural parent of the child. For an excellent discussion of this theme see: Ann Twinam, "Honor, Sexuality, and Illegitimacy in Colonial Spanish America," in *Sexuality and Marriage in Colonial Latin America,* ed. Asunción Lavrin (Lincoln: University of Nebraska Press, 1989).

9. Martínez-Alier, *Marriage, Class, and Colour,* 93–98.

10. FGEPR, Ecclesiastic Affairs. Dispensas Matrimoniales. 1815–1822.

11. FGEPR, Ecclesiastic Affairs. Dispensas Matrimoniales. 1815–1822. There is a double meaning in the Spanish term *obscura* used here. The first is of the girl being of unheralded lineage when compared to their well-documented European ancestry lines. The other is in reference to her brown skin and her African heritage.

12. FGEPR, Ecclesiastic Affairs. Dispensas Matrimoniales. 1815–1822.

13. Ibid.

14. Ibid.

15. Some official records showed María as being white and others as *parda.* This discrepancy occurred frequently in eighteenth- and nineteenth-century Puerto Rican documents.

16. FGEPR, Ecclesiastic Affairs. Dispensas Matrimoniales. 1815–1822. Unfortunately, there was no record as to whether María and Apolinario ever got married.

17. By law, a slave did not automatically become free by marrying a free person, but those free persons who married a slave more than likely hoped to set their enslaved spouses free.

18. FGEPR, Ecclesiastic Affairs. Dispensas Matrimoniales. 1815–1822.

19. For sources on free people of color in other regions see: Ira Berlin, *Slaves Without Masters: The Free Negro in the Antebellum South* (New York: Oxford University Press, 1974); Mavis C. Campbell, *The Dynamics of Change in a Slave Society: A Sociopolitical History of the Free Coloreds of Jamaica, 1800–1865* (Rutherford, NJ: Fairleigh Dickinson University Press, 1976); Edward Cox, *Free Coloreds in the Slave Societies of St. Kitts and Grenada, 1763–1833* (Knoxville: University of Tennessee Press, 1984); David W. Cohen and Jack P. Greene, *Neither Slave nor Free: The Freedman of African Descent in Slave Societies of the New World* (Baltimore: The Johns Hopkins University Press, 1972); John Hope Franklin, *The Free Negro in North Carolina, 1790–1860* (Chapel Hill: University of North Carolina Press, 1943); John D. Garrigus and Christopher Morris, *Assumed Identities: The Meanings of Race in the Atlantic World* (College Station: Published for the University of Texas at Arlington by Texas A & M University Press, 2010); Jerome Handler, *Unappropriated People: Freedmen in the Slave Society of Barbados* (Baltimore: The Johns Hopkins University Press, 1974); Gad Heuman, "White Over Brown Over Black: The Free Coloreds in Jamaican Societies During Slavery and After Emancipation," *Journal of Caribbean History* 4 (April 1981): 46–68; Jay Kinsbruner, *Not of Pure Blood: The Free People of Color and Racial Prejudice in Nineteenth-Century Puerto Rico* (Durham, NC: Duke University Press, 1996); Arnold A. Sio, "Marginality and Free Coloured Identity in Caribbean Slave Society." In *Caribbean Slave Society and Economy,* eds. Hilary Beckles and Verene A. Shepherd (New York: New Press, 1991), 150–59.

20. FGEPR, Ecclesiastic Affairs. Dispensas Matrimoniales. 1815–1822.

21. The way in which the word *mulata* was used to describe Doña María's mother in this 1836 document suggests that the author questioned the mother's character. One of the documents hints that María's parents might not have been married, which would mean María's undisclosed illegitimacy could invalidate the engagement.

22. FGEPR, Ecclesiastic Affairs. Dispensas Matrimoniales. 1815–1822.

23. Ibid.

24. Martínez-Alier, *Marriage, Class, and Colour,* 109–10.

25. Ibid., 109–12.

26. FGEPR, Ecclesiastic Affairs. Dispensas Matrimoniales. 1815–1822.

27. Ibid.

28. For more information on women of color and social and family construction see: Barbara Bush, *Slave Women in Caribbean Society, 1650–1838* (Bloomington: Indiana

University Press, 1990); David Barry Gaspar and Darlene Clark Hine, eds., *More Than Chattel: Black Women and Slavery in the Americas* (Bloomington: Indiana University Press, 1996); Suzanne Lebsock, *The Free Women of Petersburg: Status and Culture in a Southern Town, 1784–1860* (New York: Norton, 1984); Verena Martínez-Alier, *Marriage, Class and Colour in Nineteenth-Century Cuba: A Study of Racial Attitudes and Sexual Values in a Slave Society* (London: Cambridge University Press, 1974).

29. FGEPR, Ecclesiastic Affairs. Dispensas Matrimoniales. 1815–1822.
30. Ibid. The petition stated that Manuel took her into his house with an "amorous solicitation," they had three children, and now desired to legalize the union.
31. Martínez-Alier, *Marriage, Class, and Colour,* 129–30.
32. FGEPR, Ecclesiastic Affairs. Dispensas Matrimoniales. 1815–1822.
33. Ibid.
34. Ibid.
35. Martínez-Alier, *Marriage, Class, and Colour,* 103–19.
36. For discussions on the roles of women in marriage and motherhood in nineteenth-century Caribbean and Latin American society, see: Barbara Bush, *Slave Women in Caribbean Society, 1650–1838* (Bloomington: Indiana University Press, 1990); Verena Martínez-Alier, *Marriage, Class, and Colour in Nineteenth-Century Cuba: A Study of Racial Attitudes and Sexual Values in a Slave Society* (London: Cambridge University Press, 1974); Asunción Lavrin, *Sexuality and Marriage in Colonial Latin America* (Lincoln: University of Nebraska Press, 1989); Suzanne Lebsock, *The Free Women of Petersburg: Status and Culture in a Southern Town* (New York: W. W. Norton, 1985); Marietta Morrissey, *Slave Women in the New World: Gender Stratification in the Caribbean* (Lawrence: University of Kansas Press, 1989).
37. FGEPR, Political and Civil Affairs, Censo y Riqueza, caja 14.
38. Ibid.
39. Ibid.
40. This pivotal 1965 study called for true equality for black Americans at the same time it reasoned that the roots of this inequality lay in the black family itself. Beginning with the evils of slavery, the report argues the black family has been abused in ways that produced a record and a culture of family failure. The record is found in the high rates of divorce, desertion, illegitimacy, female-headed households, welfare dependency, and the culture of a mother-centered or matriarchal family, which causes high rates of delinquency, school dropout, drug use, unemployment, etc. Daniel Patrick Moynihan, *The Negro Family: The Case for National Action* (Washington D.C., 1965).
41. Frank Riessman, "In Defense of the Negro Family," In *The Moynihan Report and the Politics of Controversy,* eds. Lee Rainwater and William L. Yancey (Cambridge: MIT Press, 1966).

A Fusion of the Races: Free People of Color and the Growth of Puerto Rican Society

At the end of December 1873, mere months after the abolition of slavery, the Spanish government inquired whether the Puerto Rican military had provided arms to the people of color on the island in an effort to protect public tranquility. Perhaps remembering the concerns of Governor Prim in 1848, Spain was keen to avoid possible uprisings by recently liberated slaves within Puerto Rico, as had happened throughout the Caribbean only a few decades prior. Puerto Rican government officials replied in early January 1874 that they had not given arms to people of color, nor to anyone else, in their effort to enforce the new laws. Puerto Rico was an island of "perfect tranquility."[1] According to the officials, people of color constituted half of the population and were "in reality, more Spanish than the whites."[2] Puerto Rico, unlike its sister island of Cuba, had no antagonism between social or racial classes because "all work together, without regard to color, only to education and social position, and it can well be said that in almost the entire land there exists *a fusion of the races*."[3]

Even though this observation was made in 1874, it demonstrates an undercurrent of social thought that existed on the island throughout much of the nineteenth century. Puerto Ricans believed themselves to have a fair society based on social rank rather than racial rank. The assumption was that one could "overcome" the unfortunate circumstances of birth color by gaining economic wealth and stature within the community and by becoming educated. Regardless of the actual veracity of this assumption, there is no denying that many Puerto Ricans, both white and black, believed in the theory. This perceived social truth affected daily interactions between white Puerto Ricans and Puerto Ricans of color, while continually befuddling outsiders.

Puerto Rico's unique demographics allowed its inhabitants an opportunity to approach race relations differently. The island's free people of color and whites were not deeply divided by economic or social standards. Economically, free people of color and poor whites constituted the numerical majority on the island. Socially, free people of color and whites found a way to co-exist without the degree of fear or antagonism found elsewhere in the region. The growing sense of class and nationality on the island fostered acceptance for free people of color and recognized them as an integral part of the nineteenth-century Puerto Rican community. The lives of immigrants, natives, whites, and free people of color were fused by issues of color, class, and economics.

Limpieza de sangre ("pureness of blood"), a concept familiar to scholars of race relations in Latin America, encouraged people of African or indigenous descent to aspire to become as European as possible in style, manner, and progeny. In theory, Spanish officials required proof of *limpieza de sangre* for entrance into the university and for positions in civil bureaucracy, the Catholic Church, and the officer corps of the regular army. Government positions above a municipal hire were reserved for those with "pure" blood. Proof of this racial legitimacy required formal documentation, which was a costly and time-consuming process. Petitioners utilized local documents such as church records and community letters to petition the Crown for the right to become legally white.

We can see this legal process in action through two prominent Puerto Rican free families of color. In 1840, Don Felipe Betances of Cabo Rojo and Don Cosme Damian Delgado of Caguas filed petitions for *limpieza de sangre* with the Spanish government for "justification of the quality and cleanliness of [their] blood."[4] Both petitioners were wealthy and well-respected members of their communities. As landowners and slave owners, both men had lived in their respective communities for over twenty years. Betances, a native of Santo Domingo, established himself in Cabo Rojo as a merchant and owned a large hacienda outside of town.[5] Damian Delgado, a native of the Puerto Rican town of Caguas, owned large tracts of land in and around the mountain town. The men secured over thirty letters apiece from fellow landowners and professionals testifying to their good conduct and high social standing within their respective communities. The letters were forwarded to the Spanish government to verify their status in their communities.

If the name Betances sounds familiar to those acquainted with Puerto Rican history, it is because the scion of the family was the famous nineteenth-century scholar/physician/independence-fighter, Ramón Emeterio Betances. Ramón, who was twelve at the time of the petition, used his family's privileged social position and never shied away from his colored heritage.

Ramón always considered himself a man of color, and ideas about race and blackness became central to his visions of governance and political solidarity. Ramón was a central figure in the burgeoning Puerto Rican abolition movement and independence movement; he felt that the two movements were inseparably intertwined. He advocated for and worked with cholera patients during the island-wide epidemic of 1855 by establishing hospitals and campaigning for better sanitation practices on farms and in towns. During the same year, he was a founding member of a clandestine society dedicated to the liberation of the island's slaves. The Spanish colonial government exiled him for these activities several times.

In 1867, Ramón fled to the Dominican Republic, where he founded the Revolutionary Committee of Puerto Rico and penned *The Ten Commandments of Free Men*. With this pivotal document, Puerto Rico challenged Spain's autocratic rule. The *Commandments* demanded the abolition of slavery on the island; the inalienable rights of Puerto Rico's citizens; the rights of Puerto Ricans to assemble, bear arms, decide their own taxes, and elect their own officials; and the freedom of religion, speech, trade, and the press.[6] Seen as a champion for his fellow Puerto Ricans, regardless of their racial or civil status, Ramón Betances became known as "the father of Puerto Rican Independence."

While the future leader was still a young boy, society members from Cabo Rojo and environs collaborated to write letters of support for the senior Betances, thus revealing much about the vital role Don Felipe played in his community. One gentleman cited Betances as "a noble and virtuous citizen" while another recounted his longstanding service to the community.[7] Friends vouched for his honesty, and fellow landowners acknowledged his skill at "managing his stately *hacienda*" and its workers.[8] Betances was well-respected by his peers and appeared to be a member of their ranks, despite his partly African ancestry.

Felipe Betances challenged the Crown over the fact that he was even made to petition for his "pureness of blood." He compiled documents that demonstrated he had transcended his unfortunate circumstances of a mixed social and racial birth by educating himself and achieving prominent economic and community status for himself and his family. He revealed that while he came from a distinguished family on his maternal side, his paternal *"Betanzos"* family was *blancos llanos*, a term from the eastern regions of Hispañola referring to landless *mulatos*.[9] In eighteenth-century Dominican Republic, black or *mulato* property owners were granted elevated social and economic privileges as *blancos de la tierra* (whites of the land).[10] The landless *blancos llanos* did not hold the same privileged social status. The unequal social marriage of Don Felipe's Dominican parents launched him on the eventual path toward his petition in Puerto Rico.

The Crown manipulated the transformation of the racial heritage and the social rank of its subjects from the very beginning of the colonial era. In the personal sphere, the concept of race was fluid because Europeans, indigenous, and Africans consummated unions both inside and outside legal channels. The non-white progeny of these unions fundamentally changed the social and racial realities of the colonial hierarchical order. The clash between the private sphere and the publicly constructed reputation caused breaches in the highly stratified colonial racial and social structure by the mid–eighteenth century.

The Crown published a price schedule of favors in 1795 that essentially encouraged colonists who were considered to have any "defect," such as illegitimacy or mixed blood, to buy their way out of the problem. Colonists who found themselves saddled with a heritage of a *parda* grandparent or a non-sanctioned marriage could purchase an official edict of legitimation (*cédula de gracias al sacar*) to erase the stain of their birth.

Eligibility to gain entrance into university in the late 1700s required verification from a priest of an official *limpieza de sangre*.[11] The 1840 petition by Betances proves he accomplished the verification and completed a full course of study. Betances included a notarized documentation of graduation from the university in Santo Domingo and affidavits from university officials pronouncing him both as "white, Hispanic, and Catholic" and as an "honorable and gracious student."[12]

Since public reputation was crucial to social and racial standing *outside* the petitioner's immediate community, a petitioner had to provide substantial evidence as to how his character was perceived *inside* his particular community. Fellow neighbors of Don Cosme already saw him as a man of "certain quality" who went "beyond the call of duty" to assist his fellow citizen and his town.[13] Don Felipe must have felt it an imposition to reapply for his whiteness. Similarly, his peers in Puerto Rico stated that they did not think it "necessary for one so noble" to be "challenged in such a way."[14] Granting an edict of *limpieza de sangre* meant the Spanish Crown was validating a public reputation already acknowledged by the local community of the petitioner. Through its legislation of the *cédula*, the Crown legitimated and whitened its colonists, thereby mediating and promoting the social order within its colonies.

Don Felipe and Don Cosme were both well-respected and integral parts of Cabo Rojo and Caguas societies. Their *haciendas* were productive, they participated in civil functions, they financially supported public-works projects, and they proved they were "white" in every way but ancestry. Their petitions and the supporting documents gave every indication that they were men who, on the local level, were considered socially equal to whites, yet they clearly felt the need for their families to gain official *"calidad"* (social rank).

Outward recognition was important to this ascendant group. They worked hard to amass their wealth and reveled in the privileges of their elite status. That the Crown recognized their elite status, even in a colonial backwater like Puerto Rico, was important to their social validation. The upper classes aspired to better their situation and pushed back in small ways against anything or anyone who threatened their social position.

The aforementioned social tension must have been a concern for Don Felipe and Don Cosme to submit their petitions, because legally the need for a *limpieza de sangre* should have held diminishing significance to these families. Marriage appeared to be the central catalyst for both petitions. Both fathers had a daughter who wished to marry into prominent *blanco* families.

It is interesting to note that Betances and Delgado filed their petitions at a time when the Spanish government's interest in the procedure was waning. Two 1836 royal decrees did away with the need to supply evidence of purity of blood for most government offices. By the 1840s, notions of purity of blood became significantly less of an issue within Spain's dwindling Empire.[15] Furor over similar cases had rocked the colonies in the late eighteenth and early nineteenth centuries, causing the Spanish government to approach future petitions with circumspection and restraint. The last formal restrictions regarding *limpieza de sangre* were abolished in 1865. There is no record of the government response to either man's petition for *limpieza de sangre*.

The Alers Siblings

Thirty-year-old San Domingue native, Eugenio Alers, witnessed an incredible metamorphosis in the Caribbean region, as did many of the recent immigrants to Puerto Rico in the early nineteenth century. The island where Alers landed when he arrived in Puerto Rico in 1812 was quite different than the one from which he had sailed when he left Haiti only two short days prior. The country that he knew and loved had completely transformed and would never be the same. Civil unrest and racial strife were the norm in the newly-formed Republic of Haiti.[16] His mercantile business had little chance of succeeding when there were so few commercial goods to trade or stockpile. Weighing his options carefully, Alers chose to immigrate to Puerto Rico.

Eugenio Alers joined the wave of former French colonists who became a major force in Puerto Rico's burgeoning agricultural society. Listed as *pardo* in the immigration records, his entry is consistent with the influx of skilled people of color augmenting the labor pool in the early nineteenth century. He made cunning alliances and developed into a prosperous merchant (*comerciante*) and landowner in his adopted homeland. By 1827, the Alers family owned a large mercantile store (*comercio*) and a large house in Aguadilla's town center with six slaves to assist in the daily commercial and household tasks. He also acquired land outside of Aguadilla, which the Alers family co-owned with two other immigrant families, one white and one free colored. These families shared the land, the slaves, and the profits from their joint venture.

Alers and his main partner, Corsican immigrant Angel Luís Santini, were among the largest slave and land owners in the Aguadilla region, according to the 1838 census. Their thirty-seven slaves were between the ages of twelve and fifty years old, signaling a productive farm enterprise. Among the slaves could be found two carpenters, a mason, and a cook representing much-needed skills on a growing hacienda. The main crop was coffee, but Alers and Santini were also attempting to establish a sugar mill on the property.

In 1779, the municipality of Aguadilla had 124 *cuerdas*[17] of land in sugarcane production. By 1826, the number had increased to 779 *cuerdas* with nine new sugar-producing *haciendas* being registered. Alers and his partners rode the wave of Aguadilla's success as the region developed into a major sugar-producing district. In 1845 alone, eight new *haciendas* were registered in the municipality, and thirteen more came into existence by 1852.

By 1845, the partnership had divided their sizable assets into three *haciendas*: the Santini family remained in the Aguadilla area with almost 684 *cuerdas* of land in cultivation, Alers took his earnings and established himself on two properties in northwestern Puerto Rico, and the third partner established an hacienda in Aguada. On his property in Isabela, Alers had a total of sixty-seven *cuerdas* of land dedicated to agriculture. Twenty-five of these *cuerdas* were dedicated exclusively to sugar, and his property in Aguada was set aside for the production of coffee. He had eight slaves and four *agregados* working the property.

Eugenio was not the only success story in the Alers family. His sister, Maria Alejandrina, also owned property and slaves in the area. She emigrated from San Domingue in 1808 as a single woman [she is listed as *parda* in immigration records] and was joined four years later by her brother. Together they owned a large house in Aguada's town center, a *comercio* (large mercantile store), and an *hacienda* in Aguadilla by 1838. Maria Alejandrina was the sole proprietor of the *comercio,* and she ran it with the help of three slaves. The fourth slave, Encarnación, appeared to be her personal maid because she was listed both at the residence and at the store.

Doña Maria Alejandrina Alers sat before a notary public on August 13, 1850, concerning her relationship with Encarnación. Alers and Encarnación would play out a drama between free people of color and slaves that is rarely explored. The two apparently had an agreement that Encarnación would work toward purchasing her freedom from Alers, a legal process in the Spanish empire called *coartación*. Doña Maria was preparing her last will and testament, and within this document, she declared that when she died her slave Encarnación "*quedase coartada*" (would continue her *coartación* process) for the sum of 200 pesos.[18]

Thirteen days later, Doña Maria added a codicil to her will that would keep Encarnación in bondage until her *coartación* fee was paid in full. Alers specified the household to which Encarnación would be remanded and clarified the sum she needed to pay to acquire her freedom. The codicil indicated a 300-peso debt (100 pesos more than the previous testament).[19] Alers added that she was bestowing a home and consenting to the *coartación* after her death as payment and reward "in consideration of the good services and careful affection" rendered by Encarnación.[20]

Maria Alejandrina's brother, Eugenio Alers, acted as one of the executors of her will after her death.[21] On November 18, 1850, he sold Encarnación to Don Pedro Pablo Batistini as stipulated in the will. Don Pedro happened to be the other executor of Doña Maria's will. Encarnación was remanded to the executor for a sale price of 300 pesos as required by the will. Encarnación would reside and serve the executor until she could raise the funds to pay for her *coartación*.[22] Nearly a year later, Encarnación had still not earned her freedom. She was sold one more time with the proviso that the same probate laws regarding the price of her *coartación* would apply. There is no record as to whether or not Encarnación ever managed to pay the fee and earn her freedom.[23]

The power dynamics illustrated in the above interaction were not rare in the plantation economy. The unusual issue in this case is the convergence of both color and gender. Maria Alejandrina, a free woman of color, controlled the civil status of a fellow woman of color. She did not hesitate to adhere to the structural norms of the social order by keeping her slave in bondage and demanding, even increasing, the price of freedom. The very manner by which Maria Alejandrina adhered to the status quo demonstrates the normalcy of the system and her compliance to the values expressed by the greater society.

The white and free people of color on this "island of perfect tranquility" were truly striving to "work together, without regard to color, only to education and social position."[24] The unusual demographics peculiar to Puerto Rico allowed its inhabitants the opportunity to approach race relations differently. Free people of color and whites found a way to co-exist without the degree of fear or antagonism found in other plantation societies.

The stories of Don Felipe, Don Cosme, Don Eugenio, and Doña Maria Alejandrina demonstrate that race was not always the determinant factor in social advancement for free people of color. Persistence in endeavors and acceptance by white compatriots enabled many Puerto Rican free people of color to overcome what might have been insurmountable odds in other Caribbean plantation societies. The early

nineteenth century saw many changes both in the region and on the island, but the white and free colored inhabitants of Puerto Rico worked
steadily toward a previously unrealized compatibility. The manner by
which free people of color fit into Puerto Rican society validates the
notion of a country striving steadily toward a goal of a "fusion of the
races."

Notes

1. Archivo Historico Nacional [AHN]. Madrid. Ultramar 5103, exp. 64, 3 January
   1874 at CIH, UPR, roll 164, n.d.
2. Ibid.
3. Ibid. [emphasis mine]
4. FGEPR, Limpieza de Sangre. 1840.
5. Santo Domingo is the Spanish side of the island of Hispañola. The Dominican
   Republic gained its independence in 1844.
6. For more information on the life and work of Ramón Emeterio Betances, see:
   Ramón Emeterio Betances, *Las Antillas para los antillanos* (San Juan de Puerto Rico:
   Instituto de Cultura Puertorriqueña, 1975); Olga Jiménez de Wagenheim, *Puerto
   Rico: An Interpretive History from PreColumbian Times to 1900* (Princeton: Markus
   Wiener Publishers, 1998); Fernando Pico, *Historia General de Puerto Rico* (Río Pie-
   dras: Ediciones Huracán, 1986); Carlos M. Rama, *La independencia de las Antillas y
   Ramón Emeterio Betances* (San Juan, P.R.: Instituto de Cultura Puertorriqueña, 1980);
   Francisco A. Scarano, *Puerto Rico: cinco siglos de historia* (San Juan: McGraw-Hill,
   1993); Ada Suárez Díaz, *El doctor Ramón Emeterio Betances: Su vida y su obra* (San
   Juan de Puerto Rico: Ateneo Puertorriqueño, 1968); Ada Suárez Díaz and Ramón
   Emeterio Betances, *El doctor Ramón Emeterio Betances y la abolición de la esclavitud*
   (San Juan de Puerto Rico: Instituto de Cultura Puertorriqueña, 1980).
7. FGEPR, Limpieza de Sangre. 1840.
8. Ibid.
9. Ibid. In the petition, Don Felipe explains that perhaps some of the confusion
   regarding his status might stem from the fact that his paternal family name in
   Santo Domingo was recorded as "Betanzos."
10. It is unclear in Betatances document whether his maternal family was *blanco* or
    blanco de la tierra. Either way, his mother's social status would have been higher
    than her suitor. Information on unequal engagement proposals and marriages was
    covered in chapter four: "'Till Death Do Us Part."
11. Great examples of familial *limpieza de sangre* petitions and the requirements for
    university enrollment in the colonial era are highlighted in: Ann Twinam, "Honor,

Sexuality, and Illegitimacy in Colonial Spanish America," in *Sexuality and Marriage in Colonial Latin America*, ed. Asunción Lavrin (Lincoln: University of Nebraska Press, 1989); and Ann Twinam, *Public Lives, Private Secrets: Gender, Honor, Sexuality, and Illegitimacy in Colonial Spanish America* (Stanford, CA: Stanford University Press, 2007).

12. FGEPR, Limpieza de Sangre. 1840.

13. Ibid.

14. FGEPR. Fondo Protocols Notarial. Aguada. 1850. Paq 192.

15. Spain lost the last of its mainland colonies in 1824. By the 1836 decree, Spain's empire in the Western Hemisphere consisted only of the islands of Cuba and Puerto Rico.

16. The former French colony of San Domingue had been the most prosperous colony in the Western Hemisphere. Its agricultural-based economy was based on a brutal system of slavery that came to an abrupt end in August 1795. The colony's slaves rose in a rebellion that culminated on January 1, 1804 with the second independent republic in the Western Hemisphere, and the only successful slave revolt in the Atlantic World. For more in-depth reading on this complex and fascinating series of events, see: Laurent Dubois, *Avengers of the New World: The Story of the Haitian Revolution* (Cambridge: Belknap Press of Harvard University Press, 2004); Laurent Dubois, "Vivre Libre or Mourir!": Haiti and Guadeloupe in the Revolutionary Era," *Jamaican Historical Review* 23 (2007): 1–15; David Barry Gaspar and David Patrick Geggus, eds., *A Turbulent Time: The French Revolution and the Greater Caribbean* (Bloomington: Indiana University Press, 1997); David Patrick Geggus, ed., *The Haitian Revolution: A Documentary History* (Indianapolis: Hackett Publishing Company, Inc., 2014); David Patrick Geggus, *The Impact of the Haitian Revolution in the Atlantic World* (Columbia: University of South Carolina, 2001); David Geggus, "The Influence of the Haitian Revolution on Blacks in Latin America and the Caribbean," in *Blacks, Coloureds and National Identity in Nineteenth-Century Latin America*, ed. Nancy Priscilla Naro, (London: Institute of Latin American Studies, 2003), 38–59; David Patrick Geggus and Norman Fiering, *The World of the Haitian Revolution* (Bloomington: Indiana University Press, 2009); Gwendolyn Midlo Hall, "Saint Domingue," in *Neither Slave nor Free: The Freedman of African Descent in Slave Societies of the New World*, eds. David W. Cohen and Jack P. Greene (Baltimore: The Johns Hopkins University Press, 1972); Robert Debs Heinl, Nancy Gordon Heinl, and Michael Heinl, *Written in Blood: The Story of the Haitian People, 1492–1995* (Lanham, MD: University Press of America, 1996); David Nicholls, *From Dessalines to Duvalier: Race, Colour and National Independence in Haiti* (New York: Cambridge University Press, 1979).

17. A *cuerda* is a traditional unit of land area in Puerto Rico. It is equivalent to 3,930 square meters, 4,700 square yards, or 0.971 acres. A *cuerda* and an acre are often considered equal since they are nearly the same size.

18. FGEPR, Fondo Protocols Notarial. Aguada. 1850. Paq 192.

19. Ibid. Codicil: *"Es su voluntad que sea vendida en trescientos pesos haciéndole donación a la misma de ciento viente y cinco pesos con la condición de ir a vivir con Doña Dolores Acevedo, cuyo consorte que es el Albacea Batistini la comprara y dejara en su poder los expresados ciento viente y cinco referidos a fin de adelantarlos y que obtenga con ellos su entera libertad."*

20. FGEPR, Fondo Protocols Notarial. Aguada. 1850. Paq 192.

21. Of interest in the probate documents is the fact that Maria Alejandrina is referred to as Doña Maria, while her brother is referred to as Mr. Eugenio Alers. Both have honorifics, but the lack of a Don in front of Eugenio's name is interesting. There are some earlier census records and notarial records that list him as Don Eugenio (pre-1840); however, later records either list a Mr. Eugenio, or omit an honorific altogether. The opposite seems to occur with his sister. Earlier records omit the honorific, but post-1838 records almost all include the honorific Doña. If color is mentioned, the siblings are listed as *pardo/a* or *mulato/a*. I did find one record where Maria was record as *blanca*.

22. Nearly a year later, Encarnación had still not earned her freedom. She was sold one more time with the stipulation that the same probate laws regarding the price of her *coartación* would apply. There is no record as to whether or not Encarnación ever managed to pay the fee and earn her freedom.

23. The codicil suggests that Encarnación had already managed to raise 125 pesos of her *coartación* fee by the time she was remanded to the executor Batistini. For some reason, however, the *coartación* fee was raised from the 200 pesos quoted in the August 13 testament to the 300 pesos of the August 26 codicil. Batistini was to keep her funds on account while she raised the rest of the money for her freedom. This just demonstrates how truly difficult and frustrating the *coartación* process was for the slave. Even with legal avenues available for recourse, slaves had to contend with tax records, sales records, probate courts, and most unpredictable of all, personal piques.

24. AHN. Madrid. Ultramar 5103, exp. 64, 3 January 1874 at CIH, UPR, roll 164, n.d.

Appendix

Maps

Caribbean Region

Source: Map drawn by the Cartographic Laboratory, Department of Geography, University of Wisconsin

Puerto Rico

Source: Map drawn by the Cartographic Laboratory, Department of Geography, University of Wisconsin

Tables

Table 3–1. Populations of Free People of Color, Whites, and Slaves in the Caribbean at the End of the Eighteenth Century.[6]

Year	Colony	Free People of Color	White	Slave	Total Island Population	Free Colored Percentage of Total Island Population
1789	Martinique	5,235	10,636	83,414	96,158	5%
1789	Saint Domingue	24,848	30,831	434,424	490,108	5%
1775	Jamaica	4,500	18,700	192,800	216,000	2%
1786	Barbados	838	16,167	62,115	79,120	1%
1774	Cuba	36,301	96,440	38,879	171,620	21%
1775	Puerto Rico	34,510	29,263	7,487	71,260	48%

[6]Adapted from (Cohen and Greene, 1972, 335–39).

Table 3–2. Racial Proportions in Puerto Rico, 1779 to 1830.[1]

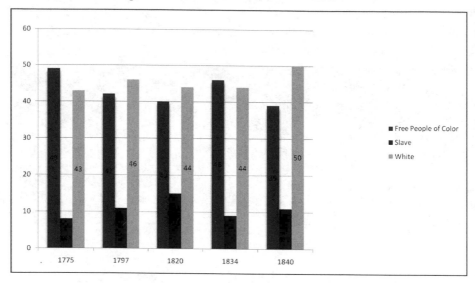

[9](Visitas, 1818–1824); (Fondo Gobernadores Españoles de Puerto Rico [FGEPR], Political and Civil Affairs. Censo y Riqueza, Caja 11–13).

Table 3–3. Free People of Color as a Percentage of the Total Population of the Country. [Blanks are indications of lack of sufficient data].[12]

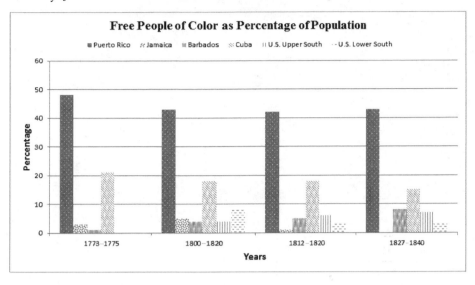

(Fondo Gobernadores Españoles de Puerto Rico [FGEPR]. Political and Civil Affairs. Censo y Riqueza. Caja 11 n.d., caja 11–13) ; (Cohen and Greene, 1972, 4–10).

Glossary

agregados – Boarders who came from the countryside and paid room and board. Often, *agregados* were relatives who came to live with family in town.

alcalde – Town magistrate, mayor.

Audiencia – Judicial arm of the Spanish colonial government that also exercised some administrative functions. Acted as an advisory board to govern and support government decisions.

Bando Contra la Raza Africana (*Proclamation against the African Race*) – Promulgated by Governor Juan Prim y Prats at the end of May 1848 as a measure to control both the free and enslaved black populations on the island. The presence of Prim y Prats and the Proclamation were short-lived in Puerto Rico, and by November 1848 both had been cast from the island.

blanco – Refers to Europeans and their white descendants who were born in the Americas.

blancos llanos – Term used in the eastern regions of Hispañola during the Spanish colonial era to refer to landless *mulatos*.

blancos de la tierra – Term used in the eastern regions of Hispañola during the Spanish colonial era. Referred to *mulatos* who owned land.

Boriquén – Taíno term for the island of Puerto Rico.

casero – Landlord or administrator.

cédula – An authorization, certificate, or official document issued throughout Spanish America by the local or overseas Spanish government.

coartación – The act of limiting or restricting slave owners' dominion over their slaves. There was no precise legal definition under Spanish law; however, it became a recognized practice in Spanish America by which a slave was able to negotiate the gradual purchase of her freedom.

cocinera – Cook.

Code Noir – Decree originally promulgated in 1685 by the French king Louis XVI. The code primarily concentrated on defining the conditions of slavery and establishing harsh controls over the enslaved.

comerciante – Owner and operator of a *comercio*.

comercio – A large mercantile store.

Costa Firme – The Spanish colonial-era province which included Venezuela, Colombia, and the isthmus of Panama.

cuerda – A traditional unit of land in Puerto Rico. It is equivalent to 3,930 square meters, 4,700 square yards, or 0.971 acres. A *cuerda* and an acre are often considered equal since they are nearly the same size.

fumacero – One who molds, shapes, and/or forms the cigar; a cigar roller.

gente de color – Term encompassing persons of mixed heritage. Translates to "people of color." The term will be used in this work to combine both *pardo* and black free people.

hacienda – A large estate or plantation used for ranching and agriculture.

Hispañola or Hispaniola – The second largest island in the Caribbean. Divided politically into the countries of Haiti and the Dominican Republic.

jornalero – A laborer who works by the day for daily wages. A hired laborer on a farm or ranch.

labradors – An agricultural laborer or small farmer.

Ley General de Jornaleros – *Jornalero* Law of 1849 forced all landless Puerto Ricans to register with governmental authorities, secure work on the farms of large landowners, and to carry *libretos* – books noting employment conditions, work records, and behavior.

Limpieza de sangre – Spanish term translated to "pureness of blood." Colonial statutes reinforced the importance of legitimate birth among certain social groups. The term began after the Reconquista as a concept of religious of purity within Iberia. It evolved into a social idea about purity of race in the Americas.

mestizo – Refers to a person of mixed indigenous and European descent.

metropole – The parent state of an overseas colony.

moreno – Refers to a person of mixed European and African heritage. The descriptor was used in Puerto Rico if the person's phenotypical appearance was more African.

mulato – Refers to a person of mixed European and African heritage.

mulatos esclavos – Refers to a slave of mixed European and African heritage. The descriptor was used in Puerto Rico if the slave's phenotypical appearance was more European.

negro – Refers to a person of African heritage. The term was used for persons of African descent with few or no apparent European features.

negros esclavos – Refers to a slave of African descent whose phenotypical appearance demonstrated few or no European features.

negros libres – Refers to a person of mixed European and African heritage who was not enslaved. The descriptor was used in Puerto Rico for a person whose phenotypical appearance demonstrated few or no European features.

Padrón de Pardos – Census of Free People of Color.

pardo – Refers to a person of mixed European and African heritage. The descriptor was used in Puerto Rico if the person's phenotypical appearance was more European.

pardos libres – Refers to a person of mixed European and African heritage who was not enslaved. The descriptor was used in Puerto Rico if the person's phenotypical appearance was more European.

peninsulares – Refers to a person of European origin who was born on the Iberian Peninsula.

Pragmática Sanción of 1776 (Pragmatic Sanction) – A decree from the Spanish Government aimed at preventing marriages of unequal caste, color, and/or class that were resulting from the allegedly ill-understood marriage codes practiced in the Spanish colonies.

quadroons – Refers to a person of mixed European and African heritage when one-quarter of their heritage can be traced to African ancestry.

Real Cédula de Gracias al Sacar of 1815 – An open invitation to people from both Europe and the Americas to settle in Puerto Rico.

San Domingue (Haiti) – Name for the French slave colony that occupied the western one-third of the Greater Antilles island of Hispañola from 1697 to 1804.

Taíno - Arawak people who were one of the major indigenous peoples of the Caribbean. Inhabitants of the islands in the Greater Antilles [Cuba, Jamaica, Hispañola, and Puerto Rico] and the northernmost of the Lesser Antilles at the time of Christopher Columbus' landing in 1492.

tornalero – Operated a lathe in colonial carpentry shops. A lathe would spin an object when pressure was applied to a pedal below the table. Carpenters could round objects such as knobs or handles by pressing their hand tools against the object while the spinning element of the lathe held the object in place.

ventorrillo – A small grocery store often run out of a room in a person's house or in a market cooperative.

Further Reading

The notes in this book give ample evidence of the richness of the field. In these selections, I will offer the interested reader additional resources for further study on a variety of topics both tangentially and more fully raised in the book. Readings include selections for foundational reading in Atlantic World, Caribbean, and Latin American history; background on the transatlantic slave trade; information on slavery in different regions of the Atlantic World; discussion on racial identity and status in Atlantic World and Latin American societies; and scholarship on free people of color throughout the Atlantic World. This listing attempts to highlight some of the important and interesting discussions in these myriad fields. It is by no means an exhaustive list of the literature.

For more background on Latin American history there are several excellent surveys, including Mark A. Burkholder and Lyman L. Johnson, *Colonial Latin America*, 7th ed. (New York: Oxford University Press, 2010); James Lockhart and Stuart B. Schwartz, *Early Latin America: A History of Colonial Spanish America and Brazil* (New York: Cambridge University Press, 1983); and John Charles Chasteen, *Born in Blood and Fire: A Concise History of Latin America*, 2nd ed. (New York: W. W. Norton, 2006).

Surveys of the history of the Caribbean region can be found in William Claypole and John Robottom, *Caribbean History. Book One: Foundations* (London: Longman Group Limited, 1989); William Claypole and John Robottom, *Caribbean History. Book Two: The Independence*, 4th ed. (London: Longman Group Limited, 2009); Nicola Foote, *The Caribbean History Reader* (New York: Routledge, 2013); Carrie Gibson, *Empire's Crossroads: A History of the Caribbean from Columbus to the Present Day* (London: Macmillan, 2014); Gad J. Heuman, *The Caribbean* (London: Hodder Arnold, 2006); B. W. Higman, *A Concise History of the Caribbean* (New York: Cambridge University Press, 2011); Tony Martin, *Caribbean History: From Pre-Colonial Origins to the Present* (Boston: Pearson, 2012); Stephan Palmié and Francisco A. Scarano, eds., *The Caribbean: A History of the Region and Its Peoples* (Chicago: University of Chicago Press, 2011); Jan Rogoziński, *A Brief History of the Caribbean: From the Arawak and Carib to the Present* (New York: Plume, 2000); and Eric E. Williams, *From Columbus to Castro: The History of the Caribbean, 1492–1969*, 4th ed. (London: A. Deutsch, 2003).

For scholarship on the Atlantic World there is a burgeoning collection of resources. Following is a list of both some of the early works in the field and some of the newer additions to the conversation. They include: David Armitage and Michael J. Braddick, eds., *The British Atlantic World, 1500–1800*, 2nd ed. (New York: Palgrave Macmillan, 2009); Bernard Bailyn, *Atlantic History: Concept and Contours* (Cambridge: Harvard University Press, 2005); Phillip Beidler and Gary Taylor, eds., *Writing Race Across the Atlantic World, 1492–1789* (New York: Palgrave Macmillan, 2002); Douglas R. Egerton, Alison Games, Jane G. Landers, Kris Lane, and Donald R. Wright, *The Atlantic World: A History, 1400–1888* (New York: Wiley, 2007); J. H. Elliott, *Empires of the Atlantic World: Britain and Spain in America, 1492–1830* (New Haven: Yale University Press, 2006); David P. Geggus, *The Impact of the Haitian Revolution in the Atlantic World* (Columbia: University of South Carolina Press, 2001); Philip Gould, *Barbaric Traffic: Commerce and Antislavery in the Eighteenth-Century Atlantic World* (Cambridge: Harvard University

Press, 2003); John R. Gillis, *Islands of the Mind: How the Human Imagination Created the Atlantic World* (New York: Palgrave Macmillan, 2009); Phyllis Whitman Hunter, *Purchasing Identity in the Atlantic World: Massachusetts Merchants, 1670–1780* (Ithaca: Cornell University Press, 2001); Colin Kidd, *The Forging of Races: Race and Scripture in the Protestant Atlantic World, 1600–2000* (New York: Cambridge University Press, 2006); Wim Klooster, *Revolutions in the Atlantic World: A Comparative History* (New York: New York University Press, 2009); Wim Klooster and Alfred Padula, *The Atlantic World: Essays on Slavery, Migration and Imagination* (Upper Saddle River, NJ: Pearson, 2004); Peter Linebaugh and Marcus Rediker, *The Many-Headed Hydra: Sailors, Slaves, Commoners, and the Hidden History of the Revolutionary Atlantic* (Boston: Beacon Press, 2001); J. R. McNeill, *Mosquito Empires: Ecology and War in the Greater Caribbean, 1620–1914* (Cambridge: Cambridge University Press, 2010); David Northrup, *Africa's Discovery of Europe 1450–1850*, 2nd ed. (New York: Oxford University Press, 2008); Mary Louise Pratt, *Imperial Eyes: Travel Writing and Transculturation*, 2nd ed. (New York: Routledge, 2007); Marcus Rediker, *Villains of All Nations: Atlantic Pirates in the Golden Age* (Boston: Beacon Press, 2005); Stuart B. Schwartz, ed., *Tropical Babylons: Sugar and the Making of the Atlantic World, 1450–1680* (Chapel Hill: University of North Carolina Press, 2004); Pamela Scully and Diana Paton, eds., *Gender and Slave Emancipation in the Atlantic World* (Durham: Duke University Press, 2005); Stephanie E. Smallwood, *Saltwater Slavery: A Middle Passage from Africa to American Diaspora* (Cambridge: Harvard University Press, 2007); Eric Robert Taylor, *If We Must Die: Shipboard Insurrections in the Era of the Atlantic Slave Trade* (Baton Rouge: Louisiana State University Press, 2009); and Alden T. Vaughan, *Transatlantic Encounters: American Indians in Britain, 1500–1776* (New York: Cambridge University Press, 2008).

A quick glimpse at materials that describe the transatlantic slave trade reveals: Robin Blackburn, *The Making of New World Slavery: From the Baroque to the Modern 1492–1800* (London: Verso, 1998); Emma Christopher, *Slave Ship Sailors and Their Captive Cargoes, 1730–1807* (New York: Cambridge University Press, 2006); Philip D. Curtin, *The Atlantic Slave Trade: A Census* (Madison: University of Wisconsin Press, 1969);

Basil Davidson, *The African Slave Trade* (Boston: Back Bay Books, 1988); Sylviane A. Diouf, ed., *Fighting the Slave Trade: West African Strategies* (Athens: Ohio University Press, 2003); David Eltis and David Richardson, eds., *Extending the Frontiers: Essays on the New Transatlantic Slave Trade Database* (New Haven: Yale University Press, 2008); David Eltis and David Richardson, *Atlas of the Transatlantic Slave Trade*, 2nd ed. (New Haven: Yale University Press, 2010); Michael A. Gomez, *Reversing Sail: A History of the African Diaspora* (Cambridge: Cambridge University Press, 2004); Herbert S. Klein, *The Atlantic Slave Trade*, 2nd ed. (New York: Cambridge University Press, 2010); and Marcus Rediker, *The Slave Ship: A Human History* (New York: Penguin, 2007).

For information specifically on the slave trade and slave markets in Latin America, see: Luiz Felipe de Alencastro, *O trato dos viventes: Formação do Brasil no Atlântico sul, séculos XVI e XVII* (São Paulo: Comphania das Letras, 2000); Laird W. Bergad, Fe Iglesias García, and María del Carmen Barcia, *The Cuban Slave Market, 1790–1880* (New York: Cambridge University Press, 1995); Joseph Calder Miller, *Way of Death: Merchant Capitalism and the Angolan Slave Trade, 1730–1830* (Madison: University of Wisconsin Press, 1988); Linda A. Newson and Susie Minchin, *From Capture to Sale: The Portuguese Slave Trade to Spanish South America in the Early Seventeenth Century* (Leiden: Brill, 2007); and Colin A. Palmer, *Human Cargoes: The British Slave Trade to Spanish America, 1700–1739* (Urbana: University of Illinois Press, 1981).

A more in-depth look at the nuances of slavery and freedom among the people of African descent in Mexico, Peru, and Cuba can be found in: Adriana Naveda Chávez-Hita, *Esclavos negros en las haciendas azucareras de Córdoba, Veracruz, 1690–1830* (Xalapa, Ver., México: Universidad Veracruzana, Centro de Investigaciones Históricas, 1987); Camillia Cowling, "'As a slave woman and as a mother': Women and the Abolition of Slavery in Havana and Rio de Janeiro," *Social History* 36, no. 3 (2011): 294–311; Christine Hünefeldt, *Paying the Price of Freedom: Family and Labor Among Lima's Slaves, 1800–1854* (Berkeley: University of California Press, 1995); Verena Martínez-Alier, *Marriage, Class, and Colour in Nineteenth-Century Cuba: A Study of Racial Attitudes and Sexual Values in a Slave Society* (London: Cambridge University Press, 1974); María

Elena Martínez, "The Black Blood of New Spain: Limpieza De Sangre, Racial Violence, and Gendered Power in Early Colonial Mexico," *The William and Mary Quarterly* 61, no. 3 (2004): 479–520; María de los Ángeles Meriño Fuentes and Aisnara Perera Díaz, "Matrimonio y familia en el ingenio, una utopía posible. Cuba (1825–1886)," *Caribbean Studies* 3, no. 1 (Jan 2006): 201–237; Michele Reid-Vazquez, *The Year of the Lash: Free People of Color in Cuba and the Nineteenth-Century Atlantic World* (Athens: University of Georgia Press, 2011); and Ben Vinson III, *Bearing Arms for His Majesty: The Free-Colored Militia in Colonial Mexico* (Stanford, CA: Stanford University Press, 2003).

Efforts to gain freedom and to exercise it were constant and multifaceted in Latin American slave societies. Works that have explored these challenges include: David W. Cohen and Jack P. Greene, eds., *Neither Slave nor Free: The Freedmen of African Descent in the Slave Societies of the New World* (Baltimore, MD: Johns Hopkins University Press, 1972); João José Reis, *Slave Rebellion in Brazil: The Muslim Uprising of 1835 in Bahia*, trans. Arthur Brakel (Baltimore: The Johns Hopkins University Press, 1993); Jane Landers, *Black Society in Spanish Florida* (Urbana: University of Illinois Press, 1999); María Elena Díaz, *The Virgin, the King, and the Royal Slaves of El Cobre: Negotiating Freedom in Colonial Cuba, 1670–1780* (Stanford, CA: Stanford University Press, 2000); Ben Vinson III, *Bearing Arms for His Majesty: The Free-Colored Militia in Colonial Mexico* (Stanford, CA: Stanford University Press, 2003); Leslie B. Rout Jr., *The African Experience in Spanish America* (1976; Princeton: Markus Wiener, 2003); and Zephyr Frank, *Dutra's World: Wealth and Family in Nineteenth-Century Rio de Janeiro* (Albuquerque: University of New Mexico Press, 2004).

Changing racial identities and status in colonial societies, spurred in part by growing free populations, are discussed in the classic work by Magnus Mörner, *Race Mixture in the History of Latin America* (Boston: Little, Brown, 1967) and more recently in: R. Douglas Cope, *The Limits of Racial Domination: Plebeian Society in Colonial Mexico City, 1660–1720* (Madison: University of Wisconsin Press, 1994); Júnia Ferreira Furtado, *Chica da Silva: A Brazilian Slave of the Eighteenth Century* (New York: Cambridge University Press, 2009); Arnold A. Sio, "Marginality and Free Coloured

Identity in Caribbean Slave Society;" in *Caribbean Slave Society and Economy*, edited by Hilary Beckles and Verene A. Shepherd (New York: New Press, 1991: 150–159); and in Ann Twinam, *Public Lives, Private Secrets: Gender, Honor, Sexuality, and Illegitimacy in Colonial Spanish America* (Stanford, CA: Stanford University Press, 1999).Here is a brief sampling of some of the scholarship on free people of color in different regions of the Atlantic World. Works on free people of color in slave societies of English-speaking North America and the British Caribbean region include: Ira Berlin, *Slaves Without Masters: The Free Negro in the Antebellum South* (New York: Oxford University Press, 1974); Sheena Boa, "Urban Free Black and Coloured Women: Jamaica, 1760–1834," *Jamaican Historical Review* 18(1993): 1–6.; Carl Campbell, "Rise of Free Colored Plantocracy in Trinidad, 1783–1813," *Bolentín de estudios latino-americanos y del Caribe* 29(1980): 35–53; Mavis C. Campbell, *The Maroons of Jamaica, 1655–1796* (Trenton: Africa World Press, Inc., 1990); Lambros Comitas and David Lowenthal, *Slaves, Free Men, and Citizens: West Indian Perspectives* (New York: Anchor, 1973); Edward Cox, *Free Coloreds in the Slave Societies of St. Kitts and Grenada, 1763–1833* (Knoxville: University of Tennessee Press, 1984); Laura Forner, "The Free People of Color in Louisiana and St. Domingue: A Comparative Portrait of Two Three-Caste Slave Societies," *Journal of Social History* 3.4 (1970): 407–30; John Hope Franklin, *The Free Negro in North Carolina, 1790–1860* (Chapel Hill: University of North Carolina Press, 1943); Jerome S. Handler, *Unappropriated People: Freedmen in the Slave Society of Barbados* (Baltimore: The Johns Hopkins University Press, 1974); Gad Heuman, "The Social Structure of the Slave Societies in the Caribbean," in *The Slave Societies of the Caribbean*, edited by Franklin Knight, Vol. 3. (UNESCO Publication, 1997); Gad J. Heuman, *Between Black and White: Race, Politics, and the Free Coloreds in Jamaica, 1792–1865* (Westport, CT: Greenwood Press, 1981); Peter H. Wood, *Black Majority: Negroes in Colonial South Carolina from 1670 through the Stono Rebellion* (New York: Norton, 1975).

Works on free people of color in the Francophone Caribbean include: Carolyn E. Fick, *The Making of Haiti: The Saint Domingue Revolution From Below* (Knoxville: University of Tennessee Press, 1990); Laura Forner, "The Free People of Color in Louisiana and St. Domingue: A Comparative Portrait of Two Three-Caste Slave Societies," *Journal of Social History* 3.4 (1970): 407–30; John D. Garrigus and Christopher Morris, *Assumed*

Identities: The Meanings of Race in the Atlantic World (College Station, TX: Published for the University of Texas at Arlington by Texas A & M University Press, 2010); Kimberly S. Hanger, *Bounded Lives, Bounded Places: Free Black Society in Colonial New Orleans, 1769–1803* (Durham: Duke University Press, 1997); Jane Landers, *Atlantic Creoles in the Age of Revolutions* (Cambridge: Harvard University Press, 2010).

Information on free people of color in Brazil is covered in: George Reid Andrews, *Blacks and Whites in São Paulo, Brazil, 1888–1988* (Madison: University of Wisconsin Press, 1991); Sidney Chalhoub, "The Precariousness of Freedom in a Slave Society (Brazil in the Nineteenth Century)," *International Review of Social History* 56, no. 03 (2011): 405–39; Carl Degler, *Neither Black Nor White: Slavery and Race Relations in Brazil and the United States* (Madison: University of Wisconsin Press, 1971); Hendrik Kraay, ed., *Afro-Brazilian Culture and Politics: Bahia, 1790s to 1990s* (New York: ME Sharpe, 1998); Herbert S. Klein, "The Colored Freedmen in Brazilian Slave Society," *Journal of Social History* 3.1 (1969): 31–45; Hebe Mattos, "'Black Troops'" and Hierarchies of Color in the Portuguese Atlantic World: The Case of Henrique Dias and His Black Regiment," *Luso-Brazilian Review* 45, no. 1 (2008): 6–29; and Katia M. de Queiros Mattoso, "Slave, Free, and Freed Family Structures in Nineteenth-Century Salvador Bahia," *Luso-Brazilian Review* 25.1 (1988): 75–84.

A sampling of works on free people of color in the Spanish Americas includes: Herman L. Bennett, *Colonial Blackness: A History of Afro-Mexico* (Bloomington: Indiana University Press, 2009); Frederick Bowser, *The African Slave in Colonial Peru, 1524–1650* (Stanford: Stanford University Press, 1974); Franklin J. Franco, *Los negros, los mulatos y la nación dominicana* (Santo Domingo, República Dominicana: Editora Manatí, 2003); Christine Hünefeldt, *Paying the Price of Freedom: Family and Labor Among Lima's Slaves, 1800–1854* (Berkeley: University of California Press, 1994); Lyman L. Johnson, "Manumission in Colonial Buenos Aires, 1776–1810," *Hispanic American Historical Review* 59.2 (1979): 258–79; Jay Kinsbruner, *Not of Pure Blood: The Free People of Color and Racial Prejudice in Nineteenth-Century Puerto Rico* (Durham: Duke University Press, 1996); Jane Landers, *Against the Odds: Free Blacks in the Slave Societies of the Americas* (London: Frank Cass, 1996); Jane Landers,

Atlantic Creoles in the Age of Revolutions (Cambridge: Harvard University Press, 2010); Suzanne Lebsock, *The Free Women of Petersburg: Status and Culture in a Southern Town* (New York: Norton, 1985); Magnus Mörner, *Race Mixture in the History of Latin America* (Boston: Little, Brown, 1967); Fernando Pico, "Esclavos, cimarrones, y negros libres en Río Piedras, 1774–1873," *Anuario De Estudios Americanos* (1986): 1–24; Michele Reid-Vazquez, *The Year of the Lash: Free People of Color in Cuba and the Nineteenth-Century Atlantic World* (University of Georgia Press, 2011); Ben Vinson III, *Bearing Arms for His Majesty: The Free-Colored Militia in Colonial Mexico* (Stanford, CA: Stanford University Press, 2003).

The age of revolution set the stage for attempts to destroy slavery altogether. Essential to understanding Latin America in the broader context of this period is Robin Blackburn, *The Overthrow of Colonial Slavery, 1776–1848* (London: Verso, 1988). For revolutionary Latin America, see: George Reid Andrews, *Afro-Latin America, 1800–2000* (New York: Oxford University Press, 2004); and Peter Blanchard, *Under the Flags of Freedom: Slave Soldiers and the Wars of Independence in Spanish South America* (Pittsburgh: University of Pittsburgh Press, 2008).

Planters held out against the revolutionary currents in the Spanish Caribbean and Brazil. On Puerto Rico, see Francisco Scarano, *Sugar and Slavery in Puerto Rico: The Plantation Economy of Ponce, 1800–1850* (Madison: University of Wisconsin Press, 1984); Christopher Schmidt-Nowara, *Empire and Antislavery: Spain, Cuba, and Puerto Rico, 1833–1874* (Pittsburgh: University of Pittsburgh Press, 1999); and Luis Figueroa, *Sugar, Slavery, and Freedom in Nineteenth-Century Puerto Rico* (Chapel Hill: University of North Carolina Press, 2005).

The former French colony of San Domingue had been the most prosperous colony in the Western Hemisphere. Its agricultural-based economy rested on a brutal system of slavery that came to an abrupt end in August 1795, culminating in the second independent republic in the Western Hemisphere, and the only successful slave revolt in the Atlantic World. For more in-depth reading on this complex and fascinating series of events, see: Laurent Dubois, *Avengers of the New World: The Story of the Haitian Revolution* (Cambridge: Belknap Press of Harvard University Press, 2004); Laurent Dubois, "'Vivre Libre ou Mourir!':

Haiti and Guadeloupe in the Revolutionary Era," *Jamaican Historical Review* 23 (2007): 1–15; David Barry Gaspar and David Patrick Geggus, *A Turbulent Time: The French Revolution and the Greater Caribbean* (Bloomington: Indiana University Press, 1997); David Patrick Geggus, *The Haitian Revolution: A Documentary History* (Indianapolis: Hackett Publishing, 2014); David Patrick Geggus, *The Impact of the Haitian Revolution in the Atlantic World* (Columbia, SC: University of South Carolina Press, 2001); David Geggus, "The Influence of the Haitian Revolution on Blacks in Latin America and the Caribbean," in *Blacks, Coloureds and National Identity in Nineteenth-Century Latin America*, edited by Nancy Naro (London: Institute of Latin American Studies, 2003: 38–59); David Patrick Geggus and Norman Fiering, eds., *The World of the Haitian Revolution* (Bloomington: Indiana University Press, 2009); Gwendolyn Midlo Hall, "Saint Domingue," in *Neither Slave nor Free: The Freedman of African Descent in Slave Societies of the New World*, edited by David W. Cohen and Jack P. Greene (Baltimore: The Johns Hopkins University Press, 1972); Robert Debs Heinl, Nancy Gordon Heinl, and Michael Heinl, *Written in Blood: The Story of the Haitian People, 1492–1995* (Lanham, MD: University Press of America, 1996); David Nicholls, *From Dessalines to Duvalier: Race, Colour and National Independence in Haiti* (New York: Cambridge University Press, 1979); and Jan Pachoński and Reuel K. Wilson, *Poland's Caribbean Tragedy: A Study of Polish Legions in the Haitian War of Independence, 1802–1803* (Boulder, CO: East European Monographs, 1986).

To understand the dismantling of slavery in the most recalcitrant slave societies, Brazil and Cuba, see Robert Edgar Conrad, *The Destruction of Brazilian Slavery, 1850–1888* (Berkeley: University of California Press, 1972); Ada Ferrer, *Insurgent Cuba: Race, Nation, and Revolution, 1868–1898* (Chapel Hill: University of North Carolina Press, 1999); Maria Helena Machado, *O plano e o pânico: Os movimentos sociais na década da abolição* (Rio de Janeiro, Brazil: Editora UFRJ; São Paulo: EDUSP, 1994); Rebecca J. Scott et al., *The Abolition of Slavery and the Aftermath of Emancipation in Brazil* (Durham, NC: Duke University Press, 1988); Rebecca J. Scott, *Degrees of Freedom: Louisiana and Cuba after Slavery* (Cambridge: Harvard University Press, 2005); Rebecca J. Scott, *Slave Emancipation in*

Cuba: The Transition to Free Labor, 1860–1899 (Pittsburgh: University of Pittsburgh Press, 2000); and Robert Brent Toplin, *The Abolition of Slavery in Brazil* (New York: Atheneum, 1971).

Information on women and the institution of marriage in colonial Latin America can be found in: Barbara Bush, *Slave Women in Caribbean Society, 1650–1838* (Bloomington: Indiana University Press, 1990; Verena Martínez-Alier, *Marriage, Class, and Colour in Nineteenth-Century Cuba: A Study of Racial Attitudes and Sexual Values in a Slave Society* (London: Cambridge University Press, 1974); Marietta Morrissey, *Slave Women in the New World: Gender Stratification in the Caribbean* (Lawrence: University of Kansas Press, 1989); Marysa Navarro, "Women in Pre-Columbian and Colonial Latin America" in *Teaching Packets for Integrating Women's History into Courses on Africa, Asia, Latin America, the Caribbean, and the Middle East* (Bloomington: Organization of American Historians, 1988); Patricia Seed, *To Love, Honor and Obey in Colonial Mexico: Conflicts Over Marriage Choice, 1574–1821* (Stanford: Stanford University Press, 1988); and Susan Socolow, "Acceptable Partners: Marriage Choice in Colonial Argentina, 1778–1810" in *Sexuality and Marriage in Colonial Latin America,* edited by Asunción Lavrin. (Lincoln: University of Nebraska Press, 1989).

For more information on the life and work of Ramón Emeterio Betances, see: Ramón Emeterio Betances, *Las Antillas para los antillanos* (San Juan de Puerto Rico: Instituto de Cultura Puertorriqueña, 1975); Olga Jimenez de Wagenheim, *Puerto Rico: An Interpretive History from PreColumbian Times to 1900* (Princeton: Markus Wiener Publishers, 1998); Fernando Pico, *Historia General de Puerto Rico* (Río Piedras: Ediciones Huracán, 1986); Carlos M. Rama, *La independencia de las Antillas y Ramón Emeterio Betances* (San Juan, PR: Instituto de Cultura Puertorriqueña, 1980); Francisco A. Scarano, *Puerto Rico: cinco siglos de historia* (San Juan, PR: McGraw-Hill, 1993); Ada Suárez Díaz, *El doctor Ramón Emeterio Betances: Su vida y su obra* (San Juan de Puerto Rico: Ateneo Puertorriqueño, 1968); Ada Suárez Díaz and Ramón Emeterio Betances, *El doctor Ramón Emeterio Betances y la abolición de la esclavitud* (San Juan de Puerto Rico: Instituto de Cultura Puertorriqueña, 1980).

Bibliography

Primary Sources

Actas Del Cabildo De San Juan De Bautista De Puerto Rico 1730–1821. Vols. 1–18. San Juan: Municipio de San Juan, 1968–1970.

Archivo General de Puerto Rico [AGPR], Fondo Gobernadores Españoles de Puerto Rico [FGEPR], Emigrados 1815–1837, caja 54.

_____ Consules y Gobiernos Extranjeros. Caracas. 1796–1821.

_____ Consules y Gobiernos Extranjeros. Cartagena. 1799–1835.

_____ Consules y Gobiernos Extranjeros. Costa Firme. 1821.

_____ Consules y Gobiernos Extranjeros. Costa Firme. 1821–1835.

_____ Consules y Gobiernos Extranjeros. Cumana. 1798–1809.

_____ Consules y Gobiernos Extranjeros. Curaçao. 1762–1838.

_____ Consules y Gobiernos Extranjeros. Guadeloupe. 1818.

_____ Consules y Gobiernos Extranjeros. Habana. 1798–1843.

_____ Consules y Gobiernos Extranjeros. Jamaica. 1810–1824.

_____ Consules y Gobiernos Extranjeros. New Orleans. 1819–1821.

_____ Consules y Gobiernos Extranjeros. Puerto Principe. 1811–1815.

_____ Consules y Gobiernos Extranjeros. San Tomas. 1762–1858.

_____ Consules y Gobiernos Extranjeros. Santo Domingo. 1796–1858.

_____ Consules y Gobiernos Extranjeros. Venezuela. 1809–1811.

_____ Ecclesiastic Affairs. Dispensas Matrimoniales. 1815–1822. Cajas 142–145.

_____ Empleos y Empleados. 1816–1850.

_____ Escalvos – Negros Libertos. 1799–1825.

_____ Escalvos – Negros Libertos. 1823–1827.

_____ Escalvos – Negros Libertos. 1824–1826.

_____ Escalvos – Negros Libertos. 1827–1837.

_____ Escalvos – Negros Libertos. 1830–1834.

_____ Escalvos – Negros Libertos. 1831–1838.

_____ Escalvos – Negros Libertos. 1838–1839.

_____ Escalvos – Negros Libertos. 1840–1847.

_____ Extranjeros. 1807–1845.

_____ Extranjeros. cajas 89–115

_____ Fiscal Affairs. Empleo. 1824–1828.

_____ Fiscal Affairs. Negros. 1828–1846.

_____ Fondo Protocols Notarial. Aguada. 1850. Paq 192.

_____ Government Agencies. Justicia. 1796–1816.

_____ Government Agencies. Justicia. 1817–1822.

_____ Government Agencies. Justicia. 1822–1824.

_____ Juez de Letras. 1821–1823.

_____ Limpieza de Sangre. 1840.

_____ Matrimonios. 1811–1820.

_____ Matrimonios. 1821–1839.

_____ Municipalities. Aguadilla. n.d.

_____ Municipalities. Añasco. n.d.

_____ Municipalities. Cabo Rojo. n.d.

_____ Municipalities. Patillas. n.d.

_____ Municipalities. Rincón. n.d.

_____ Political and Civil Affairs. Censo y Riqueza. Caja 11.

_____ Political and Civil Affairs. Censo y Riqueza. 1801–1820.

_____ Political and Civil Affairs. Censo y Riqueza. 1812–1822.

_____ Political and Civil Affairs. Censo y Riqueza. 1812–1828.

_____ Political and Civil Affairs. Emigrados.1815 –1837.

_____ Political and Civil Affairs. Censo y Riqueza." 1836–1839.

_____ Political and Civil Affairs. Censo y Riqueza. 1841–1850.

_____ Reales Órdenes 1767–1856, caja 175.

_____ Visitas. 1824.

_____ Visitas. 1818–1824.

Archivo Historico Nacional [AHN]. Madrid. Ultramar 5103, exp. 64, 3 January 1874 at CIH, UPR, roll 164, n.d.

Centro de Investigaciones Históricas [CIH], Bando Contra la Raza Africana, Leyes, Decretos, Circulares, etc. para el Gobierno de la Isla de Puerto Rico, 1833–1870, micropelícula

_____, Colección Arthur Schomburg, micropeliculas, Reel 7, Box 11

_____, Real Cédula de 1815, Leyes, Decretos, Circulares, etc. para el Gobierno de la Isla de Puerto Rico, 1814–1817, [micropelícula]

Secondary Sources

Andrews, George Reid. *Blacks and Whites in São Paulo, Brazil, 1888–1988*. Madison: University of Wisconsin Press, 1991.

Baralt, Guillermo A. *Esclavos Rebeldes: Conspiraciones y sublevaciones de esclavos en Puerto Rico, 1795–1873*. Río Piedras: Ediciones Huracán, 1982.

Bennett, Herman. *"Lovers, Family and Friends: The Formation of Afro-Mexico, 1580–1810."* Diss., Duke University, 1993.

Bergad, Laird W. *Coffee and the Growth of Agrarian Capitalism in Nineteenth-Century Puerto Rico*. Princeton: Princeton University Press, 1983.

Berlin, Ira. *Slaves Without Masters: The Free Negro in the Antebellum South*. New York: Oxford University Press, 1974.

Betances, Ramón Emeterio. *Las Antillas para los antillanos*. San Juan de Puerto Rico: Instituto de Cultura Puertorriqueña, 1975.

Boa, Sheena. "Urban Free Black and Coloured Women: Jamaica, 1760–1834." *Jamaican Historical Review* 18(1993): 1–6.

Bowser, Frederick. *The African Slave in Colonial Peru, 1524–1650*. Redwood City: Stanford University Press, 1974.

Brau, Salvador. *Historia de Puerto Rico*. Primera edición 1904. San Juan, PR: Editorial Coqui, 1966.

Bush, Barbara. *Slave Women in Caribbean Society, 1650–1838*. Bloomington: Indiana University Press, 1990.

Campbell, Carl. "Rise of Free Colored Plantocracy in Trinidad, 1783–1813." *Bolentín de estudios latino-americanos y del Caribe* 29(1980): 35–53.

Campbell, Mavis C. *The Dynamics of Change in a Slave Society: A Sociopolitical History of the Free Coloreds of Jamaica, 1800–1865*. Rutherford, NJ: Fairleigh Dickinson University Press, 1976.

_____. The Maroons of Jamaica, 1655–1796. Trenton: Africa World Press, Inc., 1990.

Chinea, Jorge L. "Race, Colonial Exploitation and West Indian Immigration in Nineteenth-Century Puerto Rico, 1800–1860." *The Americas* 54.4(1996): 495–520.

Claypole, William, and John Robottom. *Book One: Foundations*. London: Longman Group Limited, 1989.

Cohen, David W., and Jack P. Greene. *Neither Slave nor Free: The Freedman of African Descent in Slave Societies of the New World*. Baltimore: The Johns Hopkins University Press, 1972.

Coll y Toste, Cayetano. *Boletín Histórico de Puerto Rico*. Vol. 9. 14 vols. San Juan: Tipografía Cantero Fernández, 1914–1927.

Comitas, Lambros, and David Lowenthal. *Slaves, Free Men, and Citizens: West Indian Perspectives*. New York: Anchor, 1973.

Corwin, Arthur. *Spain and the Abolition of Slavery in Cuba, 1817–1886*. Austin: University of Texas Press, 1967.

Cowling, Camillia. "'As a slave woman and as a mother': women and the abolition of slavery in Havana and Rio de Janeiro." *Social History* 36, no. 3 (2011): 294–311.

Cox, Edward. *Free Coloreds in the Slave Societies of St. Kitts and Grenada, 1763–1833*. Knoxville: University of Tennessee Press, 1984.

Cruz Monclova, Lídio. *Historia de Puerto Rico (siglo XIX)*. 6 vols. Río Piedras: Editoral Universitaria, 1979.

Degler, Carl. *Neither Black nor White: Slavery and Race Relations in Brazil and the United States*. Madison: University of Wisconsin Press, 1971.

Díaz Soler, Luis M. *Historia de la esclavitud negra en Puerto Rico*. Río Piedras: Editorial Universitaria, Universidad de Puerto Rico, 1981.

_____. *Puerto Rico: Desde sus orígenes hasta el cese de la dominación española*. San Juan: Editorial de la Universidad de Puerto Rico, 1994.

Dietz, James L. *Economic History of Puerto Rico: Institutional Changes and Capitalist Development*. Princeton: Princeton University Press, 1986.

Dubois, Laurent. *Avengers of the New World: The Story of the Haitian Revolution*. Cambridge: Belknap Press of Harvard University Press, 2004.

Dubois, Laurent, and John D. Garrigus, eds. *Slave Revolution in the Caribbean, 1789–1804: A Brief History with Documents*. Basingstoke: Palgrave Macmillan, 2006.

Fick, Carolyn E. *The Making of Haiti: The Saint Domingue Revolution From Below*. Knoxville: University of Tennessee Press, 1990.

Flinter, George D. *An Account of the Present State of the Island of Puerto Rico. Comprising Numerous Original Facts and Documents Illustrative of the State of Commerce and Agriculture, and of the Condition, Moral and Physical, of the Various Classes of the Population in That Island, as Compared With the Colonies of Other European Powers; Demonstrating the Superiority of the Spanish Slave Code, - -the Great Advantages of Free Over Slave Labor, &c*. London: Longman, Rees, Orme, Brown, Green, and Longman, 1834.

Forner, Laura. "The Free People of Color in Louisiana and St. Domingue: A Comparative Portrait of Two Three-Caste Slave Societies." *Journal of Social History* 3.4 (1970): 407–30.

Franklin, John Hope. *The Free Negro in North Carolina, 1790–1860*. Chapel Hill: University of North Carolina Press, 1943.

Fuentes, Meriño, María de los Ángeles, and Aisnara Perera Díaz. "Matrimonio y familia en el ingenio, una utopía posible. Cuba (1825–1886)." *Caribbean Studies* 3, no. 1 (January 2006): 201–37.

Garrigus, John D., and Christopher Morris, eds. *Assumed Identities: The Meanings of Race in the Atlantic World*. College Station: Published for the University of Texas at Arlington by Texas A & M University Press, 2010.

Gaspar, David Barry, and David Patrick Geggus, eds. *A Turbulent Time: The French Revolution and the Greater Caribbean*. Bloomington: Indiana University Press, 1997.

Geggus, David Patrick. *The Impact of the Haitian Revolution in the Atlantic World*. Columbia: University of South Carolina, 2001.

Gómez Acevedo, Labor. *Organización y reglamentación del trabajo en el Puerto Rico del siglo XIX (propietarios y jornaleros)*. San Juan: Instituto de Cultura Puertorriqueña, 1970.

González, José Luis. *Puerto Rico: The Four-Storeyed Country and Other Essays*, trans. Gerald Guinness. Princeton: Markus Wiener, 1993.

Goveia, Elsa. *Slave Society in the British Leeward Islands at the End of the Eighteenth Century*. New Haven: Yale University Press, 1965.

_____. *The West Indian Slave Laws of the Eighteenth Century*. Barbados: Caribbean University Press, 1970.

Hall, Gwendolyn Midlo. "Saint Domingue." In *Neither Slave nor Free: The Freedman of African Descent in Slave Societies of the New World*, edited by David W. Cohen and Jack P. Greene. Baltimore: The Johns Hopkins University Press, 1972.

Hall, N. A. T. "Slave Laws of the Danish Virgin Islands in the Later Eighteenth Century." In *Comparative Perspectives on Slavery in New World Plantation Societies*, edited by Arthur Tuden and Vera Rubin. New York: New York Academy of Sciences, 1977.

Handler, Jerome S. *Unappropriated People: Freedmen in the Slave Society of Barbados*. Baltimore: The Johns Hopkins University Press, 1974.

Hanger, Kimberly S. *Bounded Lives, Bounded Places: Free Black Society in Colonial New Orleans, 1769–1803*. Durham, NC: Duke University Press, 1997.

_____. "Conflicting Loyalties: The French Revolution and Free People of Color in Spanish New Orleans." In *A Turbulent Time: The French Revolution and the Greater Caribbean*, edited by David Barry Gaspar and David Patrick Geggus. Bloomington: Indiana University Press, 1997.

Heinl, Robert Debs, Nancy Gordon Heinl, and Michael Heinl. *Written in Blood: The Story of the Haitian People, 1492–1995*. Lanham, MD: University Press of America, 1996.

Heuman, Gad. "The Social Structure of the Slave Societies in the Caribbean." In *The Slave Societies of the Caribbean*, edited by Franklin Knight. Vol. 3. UNESCO Publication, 1997.

_____. "White Over Brown Over Black: The Free Coloreds in Jamaican Societies During Slavery and After Emancipation." *Journal of Caribbean History* 4 (1981): 46–68.

Hünefeldt, Christine. *Paying the Price of Freedom: Family and Labor Among Lima's Slaves, 1800–1854*. Berkeley: University of California Press, 1994.

James, C. L. R. *The Black Jacobins: Toussaint L'Ouverture and the San Domingo Revolution 1963*. New York: Vintage, 1989.

Jiménez de Wagenheim, Olga. *Puerto Rico: An Interpretive History from Pre Columbian Times to 1900*. Princeton: Markus Wiener Publishers, 1998.

Johnson, Lyman L. "Manumission in Colonial Buenos Aires, 1776–1810." *Hispanic American Historical Review* 59.2 (1979): 258–79.

Kinsbruner, Jay. "Caste and Capitalism in the Caribbean: Residential Pattern and House Ownership Among the Free People of Color of San Juan, Puerto Rico, 1823–1846." *Hispanic American Historical Review* 70:3 (1990).

_____. *Not of Pure Blood: The Free People of Color and Racial Prejudice in Nineteenth-Century Puerto Rico*. Durham, NC: Duke University Press, 1996.

Klein, Herbert S. "The Colored Freedmen in Brazilian Slave Society." *Journal of Social History* 3.1 (1969): 31–45.

Landers, Jane. *Against the Odds: Free Blacks in the Slave Societies of the Americas*. London: Frank Cass, 1996.

_____. *Atlantic Creoles in the Age of Revolutions*. Cambridge: Harvard University Press, 2010.

Lavrin, Asunción. *Sexuality and Marriage in Colonial Latin America*. Lincoln: University of Nebraska Press, 1989.

Lebsock, Suzanne. *The Free Women of Petersburg: Status and Culture in a Southern Town*. New York: Norton, 1985.

Ledrú, Andre Pierre. *Viaje a la isla de Puerto Rico en el año 1797 de orden de su gobierno y bajo la dirección del Capitán N. Baudin*. Puerto Rico: Imprenta Militar de J. Gonzalez, 1863.

Martínez, María Elena. "The Black Blood of New Spain: Limpieza de Sangre, Racial Violence, and Gendered Power in Early Colonial Mexico," *The William and Mary Quarterly* 61, no. 3 (2004): 479–520.

Martínez-Alier, Verena. *Marriage, Class, and Colour in Nineteenth-Century Cuba: A Study of Racial Attitudes and Sexual Values in a Slave Society*. London: Cambridge University Press, 1974.

Martinez Vergene, Teresita. "The Allocation of Liberated African Labour Through the Casa De Beneficence: San Juan, Puerto Rico, 1859–1864." *Slavery and Abolition: A Journal of Comparative Studies* 12.3 (1991): 200–16.

Matos-Rodríguez, Félix M. "Street Vendors, Peddlers, Shop-Owners and Domestics: Some Aspects of Women's Economic Roles in Nineteenth-Century San Juan, Puerto Rico, 1820–1870." In *Engendering History: Caribbean Women in Historical Perspective*, edited by Verene A. Shepherd, Bridget Brereton, and Barbara Bailey. Kingston: Ian Randle, 1995.

_____. *Women and Urban Change in San Juan, Puerto Rico, 1820–1868*. Gainesville: University of Florida Press, 1999.

Mattoso, Katia M. de Queiros. "Slave, Free, and Freed Family Structures in Nineteenth Century Salvador Bahia." *Luso-Brazilian Review* 25.1 (1988): 75–84.

Morales Carrión, Arturo. *Auge y decadencia de la trata negrera en Puerto Rico, 1820–1860*. San Juan: Centro de Estudios Avanzados de Puerto Rico y el Caribe and the Instituto de Cultura Puertorriqueña, 1978.

_____. *Puerto Rico: A Political and Cultural History*. New York:W. W. Norton & Company, 1983.

Moreno Fraginals, Manuel, Frank Moya Pons, and Stanley L. Engerman, eds. *Between Slavery and Free Labor: The Spanish Speaking Caribbean in the Nineteenth Century*. Baltimore: The Johns Hopkins University Press, 1985.

Mörner, Magnus. *Race Mixture in the History of Latin America*. Boston: Little, Brown, 1967.

Morrissey, Marietta. *Slave Women in the New World: Gender Stratification in the Caribbean*. Lawrence: University of Kansas Press, 1989.

Moya Pons, Frank. *The Dominican Republic: A National History*. Princeton: Markus Weiner, 1998.

_____. *Historia Colonial de Santo Domingo*. Santiago: Universidad Católica Madre y Maestra, 1977.

Moya Pons, Frank. *La Dominación Haitian*, 3rd ed. Santiago: Universidad Católica Madre y Maestra, 1978.

Moynihan, Daniel Patrick. *The Negro Family: The Case for National Action*. Washington D.C., 1965.

Navarro, Marysa. "Women in Pre-Columbian and Colonial Latin American." *Teaching Packets for Integrating Women's History into Courses on African, Asia, Latin America, the Caribbean, and the Middle East*. Bloomington, IN: Organization of American Historians, 1988.

Naveda Chávez-Hita, Adriana. *Esclavos negros en las haciendas azucareras de Córdoba, Veracruz, 1690–1830*. Xalapa, Ver., México: Universidad Veracruzana, Centro de Investigaciones Históricas, 1987.

Nicholls, David. *From Dessalines to Duvalier: Race, Colour and National Independence in Haiti*. New York: Cambridge University Press, 1979.

Nistal-Moret, Benjamín. *Escalvos prófugos y cimarrones: Puerto Rico, 1770–1870*. Río Piedras: Editorial de la Universidad de Puerto Rico, 1984.

Parry, J. H., Philip Sherlock, and Anthony Manigot. *A Short History of the West Indies* 4th ed. London: Macmillan, 1989.

Parton, Dorothy. *The Diplomatic Career of Joel Roberts Poinsett*. Washington, DC: The Catholic University of America, 1934.

Peabody, Sue, and Tyler Stovall. *The Color of Liberty: Histories of Race in France*. Durham, NC: Duke University Press, 2003.

Pico, Fernando. "Esclavos, cimarrones, y negros libres en Río Piedras, 1774–1873." *Anuario De Estudios Americanos* (1986): 1–24.

_____. *Historia General de Puerto Rico*. Río Piedras: Ediciones Huracán, 1986.

Poinsett, Joel Roberts. *Notes on Mexico Made in the Autumn of 1822, Accompanied by an Historical Sketch of the Revolution and Translations of Official Reports on the Present State of That Country With a Map. By a Citizen of the United States*. 1824. New York: Praeger, 1969.

Rama, Carlos M. *La independencia de las Antillas y Ramón Emeterio Betances*. San Juan: Instituto de Cultura Puertorriqueña, 1980.

Ramos Mattei, Andrés. *Azúcar y esclavitud*. San Juan: Ediciones Huracán, 1982.

Reid-Vazquez, Michele. *The Year of the Lash: Free People of Color in Cuba and the Nineteenth-century Atlantic World*. Athens: University of Georgia Press, 2011.

Riessman, Frank, "In Defense of the Negro Family." In *The Moynihan Report and the Politics of Controversy*, edited by Lee Rainwater and William L. Yancey. Cambridge: MIT Press, 1966.

Rippy, James and Joel R. Poinsett. *Versatile American*. Durham, NC: Duke University Press, 1935.

Roberts, J. M. *A History of Europe*. New York: Allen Lane, 1996.

Rodríguez San Pedro, Joaquín. *Legislación ultramaria*. Vol. 5. Madrid: Imprenta Manuel Minuesa, 1868.

Russell-Wood, A. J. R. "Colonial Brazil." In *Neither Slave nor Free: The Freedman of African Descent in Slave Societies of the New World*, edited by Jack P. Cohen and David W. Greene. Baltimore: The Johns Hopkins University Press, 1972.

San Juan, Municipio de. "Actas Del Cabildo De San Juan De Bautista De Puerto Rico, 1730–1821." Vols. 1–18. *San Juan: Municipio de San Juan*, 1968–1970.

Scarano, Francisco A. *Puerto Rico: cinco siglos de historia*. San Juan: McGraw-Hill, 1993.

_____. *Sugar and Slavery in Puerto Rico: The Plantation Economy in Ponce, 1800–1850*. Madison: University of Wisconsin Press, 1984.

Scott, Rebecca J. *Slave Emancipation on Cuba: The Transition to Free Labor, 1860–1899*. Princeton: Princeton University Press, 1990.

Seed, Patricia. *To Love, Honor and Obey in Colonial Mexico: Conflicts Over Marriage Choice, 1574–1821*. Redwood City: Stanford University Press, 1988.

Sio, Arnold A. "Marginality and Free Coloured Identity in Caribbean Slave Society." In *Caribbean Slave Society and Economy*, edited by Hilary Beckles and Verene A. Shepherd. New York: New Press, 1991.

Smith, Justin. *Poinsett's Career in Mexico*. Worcester, MA: American Antiquarian Society, 1914.

Socolow, Susan. "Acceptable Partners: Marriage Choice in Colonial Argentina, 1778–1810." In *Sexuality and Marriage in Colonial Latin America*, edited by Asunción Lavrin. Lincoln: University of Nebraska Press, 1989.

Sterling, Philip, and Maria Brau. *The Quiet Rebels: Four Puerto Rican Leaders*. New York: Doubleday, 1968.

Suárez Díaz, Ada. *El doctor Ramón Emeterio Betances: Su vida y su obra*. San Juan de Puerto Rico: Ateneo Puertorriqueño, 1968.

Suárez Díaz, Ada and Ramón Emeterio Betances. *El doctor Ramón Emeterio Betances y la abolición de la esclavitud*. San Juan de Puerto Rico: Instituto de Cultura Puertorriqueña, 1980.

Sued Badillo, Jalil, and Angel Lopez Cantos. *Puerto Rico negro*. Río Piedras: Editorial Cultural, 1986.

Sonesson, Birgit. *La real hacienda en Puerto Rico: Administración, política y grupos de presión (1815–1869)*. Madrid: Instituto de Estudios Fiscales & Instituto de Cooperación Iberoamericana, 1990.

Twinam, Ann. "Honor, Sexuality, and Illegitimacy in Colonial Spanish America." In *Sexuality and Marriage in Colonial Latin America*, edited by Asunción Lavrin. Lincoln: University of Nebraska Press, 1989.

_____. *Public Lives, Private Secrets: Gender, Honor, Sexuality, and Illegitimacy in Colonial Spanish America*. Stanford, CA: Stanford University Press, 2007.

Vinson, Ben. *Bearing arms for his majesty: The free-colored militia in colonial Mexico*. Stanford, CA: Stanford University Press, 2003.

Wagenheim, Kal. *Puerto Rico, Its History and Culture*. Elizabethtown, PA: Continental Press, 1989.

Wagenheim, Kal, and Olga Jiménez de Wagenheim. *The Puerto Ricans: A Documentary History*. Princeton: M. Wiener Publishers, 1994.

Williamson, Edwin. *The Penguin History of Latin America*. New York: Penguin, 1992.

Wood, Peter H. *Black Majority: Negroes in Colonial South Carolina From 1670 Through the Stono Rebellion*. New York: Knopf, 1974.

Zamora y Coronado, José María. *Biblioteca de legislación ultramarina en forma de diccionario alfebeto*. Madrid, 1845.

Index

ROCHELLE BROCK &
RICHARD GREGGORY JOHNSON III,
Executive Editors

Black Studies and Critical Thinking is an interdisciplinary series which examines the intellectual traditions of and cultural contributions made by people of African descent throughout the world. Whether it is in literature, art, music, science, or academics, these contributions are vast and far-reaching. As we work to stretch the boundaries of knowledge and understanding of issues critical to the Black experience, this series offers a unique opportunity to study the social, economic, and political forces that have shaped the historic experience of Black America, and that continue to determine our future. Black Studies and Critical Thinking is positioned at the forefront of research on the Black experience, and is the source for dynamic, innovative, and creative exploration of the most vital issues facing African Americans. The series invites contributions from all disciplines but is specially suited for cultural studies, anthropology, history, sociology, literature, art, and music.

Subjects of interest include (but are not limited to):

- EDUCATION
- SOCIOLOGY
- HISTORY
- MEDIA/COMMUNICATION
- RELIGION/THEOLOGY
- WOMEN'S STUDIES

- POLICY STUDIES
- ADVERTISING
- AFRICAN AMERICAN STUDIES
- POLITICAL SCIENCE
- LGBT STUDIES

For additional information about this series or for the submission of manuscripts, please contact Dr. Brock (Indiana University Northwest) at brock2@iun.edu or Dr. Johnson (University of San Francisco) at rgjohnsoniii@usfca.edu.

To order other books in this series, please contact our Customer Service Department:

(800) 770-LANG (within the U.S.)
(212) 647-7706 (outside the U.S.)
(212) 647-7707 FAX

Or browse online by series at www.peterlang.com.